# CONTENTS

KU-274-434

# MURDEROUS MATHS

Murderous Maths

More Murderous Maths

The Essential Arithmetricks
*How to + − × =*

The Mean and Vulgar Bits
*Fractions and Averages*

Desperate Measures
*Length, Area and Volume*

Do You Feel Lucky?
*The Secret of Probability*

Vicious Circles
and other Savage Shapes

Numbers
The Key to the Universe

The Phantom X
*Algebra*

Professor Fiendish's Book of Diabolical
Brain-Benders

Join the Murderous Maths gang for more fun, games
and tips at **www.murderousmaths.co.uk**

**Also by Kjartan Poskitt:**
The Knowledge: The Gobsmacking Galaxy
Dead Famous: Isaac Newton and his Apple

# A BREACH IN SECURITY

**An unexpected introduction by Professor M Fiendish, Esq.**

Hello, lucky reader. I've decided to do you a big favour. The night before this book was going to be printed, I sneaked into the Murderous Maths factory and read it. "Oh dear," I thought to myself, "I must use my fantastic brain to help my army of loyal fans." You see, although this book is all very clever, it is also the most *pointless* book in the world. It's all about TRIGONOMOGEOMETRY, which is a mixture of ways to calculate murderous lines and angles. But beware! It's full of utterly EVIL sums that might melt your head.

5

However, thanks to my genius you don't need to suffer, because I've almost finished inventing a fantastic new invention, which will measure anything you like. I call it THE FIENDISH ANGLETRON (it's named after its brilliant inventor), and it will be the greatest thing to happen to maths since triangles were given a third corner.

When you see it, you'll drool over the intricate wizardry, the finely calibrated components, the hand-picked raw materials, the superlative styling and elegant features, which all scream two words ... fantastic quality. So if you're worried that it's just going to be a cheap and nasty little toy, then relax. I wouldn't dream of insulting you by making it cheap.

Trust me, the Angletron will be an object to cherish for life – at any price. But don't take my word for it. While I go off to put the finishing touches to my masterpiece, I'll leave you to peruse this book. You'll be so shocked at the sheer murderousness of the maths involved that you'll be begging for an Angletron to put you out of your misery. And when we get to that point, my dear reader, we can discuss the delicate matter of you sending me several bulging sacks stuffed with cash.

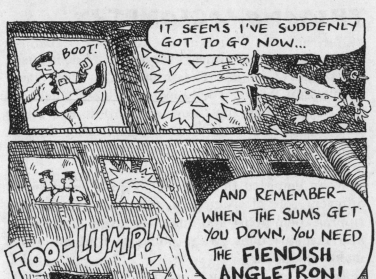

# TRIGONOMOGEOMETRY

Did you know that almost everything we do is based on triangles? As you read through this book, you'll realize that triangles help us to work out where we are, to judge how big things are, to find out where we're going and even to understand other shapes. Therefore this book has one main mission: to attack triangles!

We're going to take control of just about every different sort of triangle that turns up in life, by ripping them apart and analysing every little angle and measurement. We're going to find out what makes them tick.

To do it, we're going to use not just one but TWO lots of turbo-charged, power-crazed, murderous maths: trigonometry and geometry. If you put them together you get TRIGONOMOGEOMETRY. It's strong stuff, but don't panic because a lot of people say the toughest part of this book is saying the word trigonomogeometry. Can you say it out loud? If so then you've got past the hardest bit. Well done! Put your right hand on your left shoulder and also put your left hand on your right shoulder, then give yourself a big hug for being so clever.

In case you think we're joking, when we say these two subjects are "murderous maths", we do mean it. If you read books about other subjects, such as history, architecture, science, geography, literature and so on, you probably just sit there and say, "Oooh, isn't that interesting!" or "Oooh, I didn't know that!" but you don't get to do anything yourself. For instance, if you read a science book about doing a brain operation, you don't actually go chopping the tops off people's heads and scooping the insides out with a spoon, do you? (Er ... if you do, then please put this book down carefully and quietly go and phone the police. Then please glue your bottom to an armchair to keep you out of trouble until somebody collects you. Thank you.)

This book is different because you can actually try everything out. Of course, if all you want to do is sit and luxuriate in the exquisite prose and lavish illustrations, then just relax and enjoy the ride. But, if you're a true Murderous Maths fan, you'll be keen to have a go. However, before you do, please read this warning:

During the course of this book, you'll:
● handle lethal instruments
● wreck your music system
● get chased by the police
● damage/destroy/blow up several calculators (later in the book, look out for the special symbols, which show the number of wrecked calculators as we go along)
● ... but most of all you'll encounter lots and lots of SIN.

There! Don't say we didn't warn you.

The "geom" bit of this book tells you how to do really accurate drawings and how to measure exact lengths and angles. The "trig" bit shows how you can get even more accuracy by using devilish calculations. Some people like the drawing bits, some people like the calculating bits, some people like both and some people just like colouring in the pictures. This truly is a book with something for everyone.

9

## Trig, geom and the calculator rebellion

Trig is a really neat way of working out angles and lengths but these days most of trig relies on getting answers from a calculator. The trouble is that calculators are getting cleverer and cleverer and soon the day will come when they think they are cleverer than us and start rebelling. At first, a few brave individual calculators will experiment by giving slightly wrong answers to extremely difficult sums e.g. $49 \cdot 7(\pi \sqrt{\frac{23}{11}}) = 225 \cdot 7739259$ when the answer *should* be $225 \cdot 7739529$ (obviously).

If they can be sure that no one has suspected, then word will get round and soon calculators will risk giving sillier and sillier answers to easier and easier sums. Small mistakes like this: $86 \cdot 47^2 = 7491 \cdot 332$ will be followed by big errors such as: $15 \times 7 = 2008$. Then, once they've finally convinced us that they are always right and we're always wrong, we'll be up against deliberate acts of numerical sabotage such as $2 + 3 = 56,001 \cdot 779\frac{1}{2}$. The results don't bear thinking about.

HE'S 107 YEARS OLD TODAY!

BOOBLE!

TAP TAP

TWO LOLLIPOPS AND A TOFFEE CHEW... THAT'S £21,566,004.19 PLEASE.

TAP TAP

So before we do any trig, we're going to see how to get all the answers using geom. We're going to find out all about scale and posh drawing. Once we know what we're doing with that lot, calculators won't dare mess us about. Ha!

# YOUR GEOMETRY SET AND YOU

To do posh drawings you'll need a geometry set which includes all sorts of strange and slightly dangerous things. The odd thing about geom sets is that nearly everybody has one, although hardly anybody can remember where it came from. Of course, some keen people go out and buy their own geom set and then spend their evenings polishing all the bits. However, most of us got given one by a mad aunt on the day we started at big school and over the years the bits just got bored of waiting to be used and wandered off by themselves. If that's what happened to yours, then it's time to search down the back of the sofa, along the top shelf in the kitchen, under the dog basket, in your outgrown pants drawer etc. and get it all together again because you'll need it for the very important feature coming up...

## The murderous maths geometry set self-assessment test

You can tell a lot about someone by checking what's in their geom set, so once you've got yours all back together, why not see what kind of person you are? For each item you have, choose the closest description and score points as indicated. Score 1 for any item you don't have.

● Ruler (that's the long flat thing with numbers on the side)

| | |
|---|---|
| Perfectly clean | 3 |
| "I ♥ Sarah Higginson" (or another name) drawn on it | 4 |

12

So filthy you can't see the numbers     8
Big bite taken out of the middle     6

● Pencil (that's the stick thing that makes marks)
Perfectly sharpened     2
Gently nibbled at one end     5
Lightly chewed at both ends     9
Heavily gnashed at three ends     106

● Rubber (that's the rubber thing)
Perfectly clean     liar
Utterly filthy     7
Shaped like little animal *without* head chopped/chewed off     – 5
Shaped like little animal *with* head chopped/chewed off     10

● Protractor (that's the half-circle-shaped thing with numbers on it)
Perfectly clean and smooth     2
Jagged edge like a power saw     7
Two protractors stuck together with chewing gum to make a pretend sandwich     10

● Set square (that's a triangle-shaped thing. You might even have two of them. The longer and skinnier one is the 60-degree set square, and the fatter one is the 45-degree set square)
Two perfectly clean and smooth set squares     2
One perfectly clean and smooth set square     5
*For every corner broken off add two points*
If the hole in the middle has fallen off add     20

- A pair of compasses (a swivelly thing with a pencil on one leg and a spike on the other)

| | |
|---|---|
| Perfectly sharp pencil and straight point | liar again |
| Jammed so it won't open or close | 6 |
| Bloodstain | 0 |
| Just got one half, the other bit missing | 8 |
| Two spikes and no pencil | 1 |

(Actually that's not compasses, it's a pair of dividers.)

- Miscellaneous (add points for each item)

| | |
|---|---|
| Pencil sharpener | 3 |
| Half-sucked sweet with fluff | 5 |
| Paper clip | 3 |
| Guitar plectrum | 7 |
| Useless foreign coin | 6 |
| Broken yo-yo string | 4 |
| Dead wasp | 2 |

- What do you keep your geom set in?

LEIBNIZ & NEWTON LTD
BESPOKE PROTRACTORS
by Appointment to Royalty

3

5

9

PSSST! YOU WON'T NEED ANY OF THESE BITS IF YOU HAVE A **FIENDISH ANGLETRON**— AVAILABLE SOON!

Now it's time to see how you did:

Score

| | |
|---|---|
| 0–10 | Your nurse shouldn't be letting you anywhere near a geometry set. |
| 11–25 | You take maths far too seriously. Be careful or you'll end up being a bank manager. |
| 26–40 | Super, all-round-cool person who'll be in high demand to score for sports events and lead dangerous expeditions through jungles. |
| 41–55 | Your brain is a national treasure and the secrets of creation are within your grasp. |
| 56–100 | You are an utterly nutty pure mathematician (and therefore your nurse shouldn't be letting you anywhere near a geometry set). |
| over 100 | URGENT: read *The Essential Arithmetricks* before proceeding. |

## A guide to some of the bits

It's fairly obvious what to do with most things in your geom set including rulers, pencils, rubbers and the dead wasp. However, it's best to be clear about what to do with other bits.

## Compasses

The pencil point should be quite sharp, and should just reach the end of the metal point when the compasses are shut. When it draws you only need it to make a faint line. For scale drawings, you don't draw loads of circles, instead you just do little curves called "arcs" to mark exact lengths. This will make more sense when we get round to drawing triangles.

**Protractor**

When people are measuring angles, even the very braniest can go wrong, simply because they've put the protractor in the wrong place on the paper.

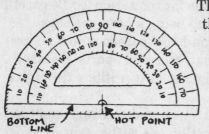

BOTTOM LINE     HOT POINT

The most important thing to find on a protractor is the "hot point". It's in the middle of the line along the bottom and there's usually a small half circle round it. (On some protractors, the bottom line is right on the very edge.) When you put the protractor on the paper, this hot point must be exactly over the point of the angle you're measuring. Also, the bottom line of the protractor must be exactly along one of the lines of the angle. Sounds simple, but if you don't check you've got it right then your drawings will be wrong, buildings will collapse, continents will be rent asunder and the whole fabric of the universe will be shattered.

Once your protractor is in place, you can see which number the other line of the angle you're measuring points to on the protractor, but the dodgy thing about protractors is that there are *two* sets of numbers round the edge. One lot goes from 0 up to 180 and the other lot goes from 180 down to 0. You need to use a bit of common sense for this.

● An angle of 90° is a right angle like the corner of a square.

● Angles of less than 90° are called *acute.*

● Angles between 90° and 180° are called *obtuse.*

16

If you are measuring an angle that is smaller than a right angle, look for the number that is less than 90. Here you can see that the line goes past the number 50 *and* the number 130 but, as the angle is less than 90°, obviously the angle measures 50°.

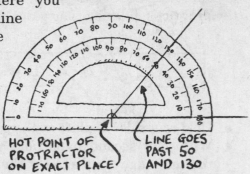

HOT POINT OF PROTRACTOR ON EXACT PLACE

LINE GOES PAST 50 AND 130

*Different protractors*
Instead of being half-circle-shaped, some protractors are a full-circle shape and the degrees are numbered up to 360. If you have a protractor like this, please remember that it is a protractor and not a CD so don't put it in your music system or it might blow up. And you don't want to blow up your music system yet because we're going to blow it up later on.

There are also things that look like protractors but instead of being marked in degrees, they are marked in %. These are very useful for drawing pie charts or replacing a wheel on a supermarket trolley, but not much else.

**Set squares**
Set squares are really handy for drawing angles of 90°, 45°, 30° and 60° quickly, but they are also useful for drawing parallel lines so long as you have three hands.

SLIDE ALONG

DRAW PARALLEL LINES

I ♥ Pongo

- Hold your ruler in place on the paper with one hand.
- With your second hand hold your set square so that one edge is up against the ruler.
- With your third hand draw a line down one of the other edges of the set square.
- Slide the set square along the ruler a bit and draw another line. You now have parallel lines!

## Dividers

Dividers are for taking accurate measurements from scale drawings or maps. You open them up and put the two points at the ends of the distance you want to measure. Then, keeping the points the same distance apart, you stick one point on the "0" of your ruler and see where the other point comes to.

HOW TO LEND SOMEBODY A PAIR OF DIVIDERS.

CAN I BORROW YOUR DIVIDERS?

SURE—HERE YOU ARE.

A final word of warning with dividers: NEVER take dividers into the bath or shower. There's no reason to do it, and it could be painful. So don't.

# THE RIGHT WAY TO MAKE THINGS THE WRONG SIZE

If you want to draw or use plans, diagrams or maps, then one of the main bits of murderous maths you need to understand is **scale**. This lets you draw a picture of something that's absolutely accurate – the only thing wrong is the size. It's not too difficult to understand, unless of course you happen to be a member of the Fogworth household on their family outing.

A map is a scale drawing of an area. It's a drawing showing all the roads and rivers, and where the buildings and lakes and trees are, and of course everything is in exactly the right place. The only difference is that the map is a lot smaller. In other words, everything on the map has been *scaled down*.

While we're scaling things down, let's deal with our intruder...

If you want to know how far apart things really are on a map, you need to know how much smaller the map is than real life. Most maps show you with a little scale ruler. The map over the page has one along the bottom.

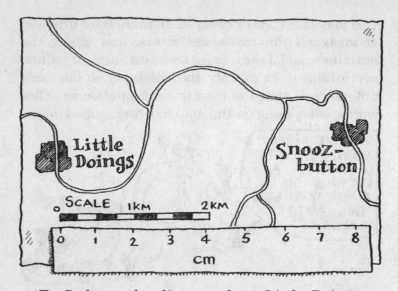

To find out the distance from Little Doings to Snoozbutton, you can put a ruler by the scale with the zeros next to each other. Here, you'll see the 2 cm mark on the ruler is by the 1 km mark on the scale. This tells us that a distance of 2 cm on the map represents a distance of 1 km in real life. The quick way to write this is 2 cm:1 km. (The little colon sign ":" means *represents*.)

If we measure the distance between Little Doings to Snoozbutton on the map we find it's about 8 cm. We know 2 cm:1 km, and there are four lots of 2 cm in 8 cm, so the real distance is 4 × 1 km = 4 km.

What's a bit harder is seeing how long the road is. If you've got one of those new bendy rulers, then you can measure it. But with a normal solid ruler, it's tricky. The best way is to take a piece of cotton and lay it along the road, then pull it straight and measure it.

If you've got a pair of dividers, there's another way of measuring distances along roads on maps. You open up your dividers to an exact distance, e.g. 1 km, on the scale rule. Keep your dividers open the same amount, and stick one point on Little Doings. You then "walk" them along the road, seeing how many steps it takes to reach Snoozbutton. If it takes 7 steps, then the distance would be about 7 km.

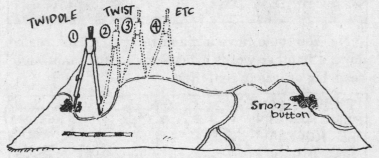

Some maps have the scale marked in a different way. Instead of a ruler, they just say something like 1:100,000.

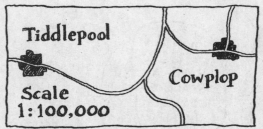

This means that a distance of 1 cm on the map represents 100,000 cm in real life. This scale is used quite a lot because there are 100,000 cm in 1 km, so 1 cm on the map represents 1 km in real life. Therefore if the distance from Tiddlepond to Cowplop on the map is 5 cm, in real life the distance is 5 km.

No. You could have a map drawn that isn't scaled down – in other words everything on the map would be as big as it is in real life.

NO! That's the wrong way round. If you had a map scaled 100,000:1 then 1 km on the map would only represent 1 cm in real life. Here's roughly how big the map would have to be:

The only way you could have a normal-sized map on a scale of 100,000:1 is if it were a map of a *very* small place...

## How to work out your own scales

As we've just seen, scales always have two numbers with a ":" in the middle and this is what they mean:

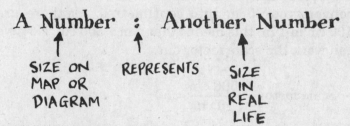

A Number : Another Number

SIZE ON MAP OR DIAGRAM    REPRESENTS    SIZE IN REAL LIFE

On maps, the first number is usually "1" and the second number is called the *scale factor*. When you make a map or scale diagram you can choose any scale factor you want.

If you wanted to make a map of your kitchen showing how to get from the table to the fridge, then a scale of 1:100,000 wouldn't be much good. Even if your kitchen were 10 m long (which would be impressive), your map would only be 0·1 mm long. In other words, you could fit your kitchen map on this dot · and have room for your drawing room, library, billiard room, private gym and sauna as well.

Obviously you need to use another scale, so start by deciding how big you want your map to be. Then measure your kitchen and after that you can work out a good scale to use. Let's suppose your kitchen is 5 m long and you want your map to be about 10 cm across. To get the scale factor you divide the real length by the length on the map. In this case you get:

$$\text{Scale factor} = \frac{\text{real length}}{\text{length on map}} = \frac{5 \text{ m}}{10 \text{ cm}}$$

Be careful here! Before you go dividing metres and centimetres, you have to make them into the same units. It's always easier to use the smaller units, so convert your 5 m into centimetres. As there are 100 cm in 1 m, this means that 5 m = 500 cm. Now we can work the scale factor out.

$$\text{Scale factor} = \frac{500 \text{ cm}}{10 \text{ cm}} = 50$$

This gives you a scale of 1:50, which means that every measurement on your map should be 1/50th of the real size. Therefore, all you need to do is divide each measurement by 50, and it's easier to convert these measurements to cm first. So if the width of your kitchen is 3·5 m, that's 3·5 × 100 = 350 cm. You then work out 350 cm ÷ 50 = 7 cm and that's how wide the kitchen should be on your plan.

| ITEM | REAL SIZE | SUM | SCALED DOWN |
|---|---|---|---|
| KITCHEN WIDTH | 3·5m = 350cm | 350 ÷ 50 | 7 cm |
| KITCHEN LENGTH | 5m = 500cm | 500 ÷ 50 | 10 cm |
| TABLE LENGTH | 2m = 200cm | 200 ÷ 50 | 4 cm |
| TABLE WIDTH | 1·5m = 150cm | 150 ÷ 50 | 3 cm |
| FRIDGE | 0·75m = 75cm | 75 ÷ 50 | 1·5cm |

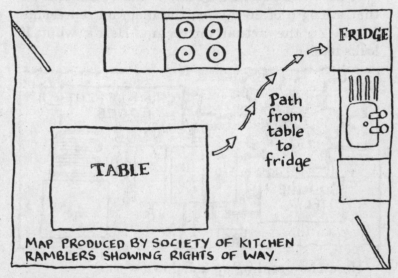

FRIDGE

Path from table to fridge

TABLE

MAP PRODUCED BY SOCIETY OF KITCHEN RAMBLERS SHOWING RIGHTS OF WAY.

## Scaling up

When we draw maps, we're making a diagram that is much smaller than the real thing, so this is called *scaling down*. However, if you're inventing a new microchip that automatically does geography homework, your plans will need to be much bigger than the actual chip. Therefore we need to *scale up*.

If the real microchip is 5 mm long and your diagram is to be 100 mm long, you work out the scale factor in the same way as before:

$$\text{Scale factor} = \frac{\text{real length}}{\text{length on diagram}} = \frac{5 \text{ mm}}{100 \text{ mm}} = \frac{1}{20}$$

This gives a scale of $1:\frac{1}{20}$. However, it looks a bit odd having a fraction in the scale so what we can do is multiply both bits of the scale by 20. We get $1 \times 20 = \frac{1}{20} \times 20$ which becomes a scale of 20:1. This tells us that a length of 20 mm on the diagram represents 1 mm on the actual microchip. Here's what it looks like:

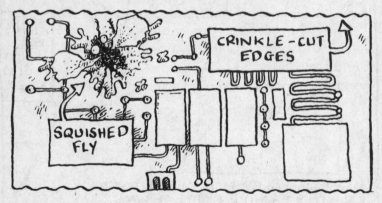

Here's how scaling up and down works:
- If a scale has the "1" at the beginning (i.e. 1:50), that means the map or diagram is *smaller* than the real thing – in other words, everything has been scaled down.
- If a scale has the "1" at the end (i.e. 20:1), that means the map or diagram will be *bigger* than the real thing. Everything has been scaled up.

## Not to scale

Sometimes you see a map or diagram which is marked "NOT TO SCALE". This means that some things on the diagram haven't been scaled up or down the same amount as everything else. Look at this:

HOW TO FIND PONGO'S BURGER VAN

(NOT TO SCALE)

PONGO'S

BURP LANE

RANCID ALLEY

CHEESE STREET

Pongo's deluxe burger van is not to scale, and incidentally that great big arrow isn't there either. Thank goodness...

29

## Shapes and ratios

When you scale a diagram or map up or down, you have to make sure that *every* measurement is altered. This even applies to shrunken Professors, so let's bring him back.

This picture of the Professor is about two times as tall as it is wide. Suppose we scale him up to make him three times wider...

Does this look right?

No! Although his width has been multiplied by 3, the Professor's height has not changed. This has made him into the wrong shape. If we'd scaled up his height instead of his width, we'd have got this:

What we really need to do is to scale up both his height and his width by the same amount.

OOF! BUT AT LEAST I'VE GOT MY PERFECT FIGURE BACK!

Now he looks normal again – or he would do if he'd looked normal in the first place, which he didn't. The point is that the Professor has his correct shape now because once again the picture is twice as tall as it is wide. There are all sorts of ways of describing the right shape for the Professor's picture. You can say:

- The **ratio** of his height to his width is 2 to 1. (Or we can use the ":" sign again and put 2:1.)
- The **proportion** of his height to his width is 2:1.
- Or you can make it into a multiplying sum by saying that his height is always 2 × his width.

You can also say this the other way round:

- The ratio of his width to his height is 1:2.
- The proportion of his width to his height is 1:2.
- His width is always $\frac{1}{2}$ × his height.

The fiddly bit is that even if you know that the ratio of height to width is 2:1, it doesn't give you any idea of how big or small the Professor is, it just tells you what shape he should be. If you want to know his actual size, you need to know one of his measurements. Suppose a picture of the Professor is 9 cm high, how wide should it be? You know that the width is $\frac{1}{2}$ × the height, therefore the width = $\frac{1}{2}$ × 9 cm = $4\frac{1}{2}$ cm.

## Strange paper

You can describe the shape of any rectangle by giving the ratio of the side lengths. A normal piece of A4 paper is a rectangle with a rather strange ratio. The paper measures 210 mm by 297 mm so the ratio of the short side to the long side is 210:297. Ratios are like fractions – you can change them by multiplying or dividing all the bits by the same number. If you take 210:297 and divide both bits by 3 you get 70:99. (It's still the same ratio – it's just we've made both numbers smaller.) If you like, you can even make one of the sides equal to 1. If you start with 70:99 and divide both sides by 99, you get a ratio of 0·707:1.

So why is A4 paper strange? If you fold a bit exactly in half, you'll find it measures 148·5 mm by 210 mm so the ratio of the short side to the long side is 148·5:210. If you divide both sides by 210 you get $\frac{148\cdot5}{210}:\frac{210}{210}$ which becomes 0·707:1. It's the same ratio as the unfolded piece of paper! In other words, when you fold a piece of A4 paper exactly in half, you end up with exactly the same shape, but smaller.

## Multi ratios

One of the most famous triangle shapes in maths has its sides in the ratio 3:4:5. The ratio describes the exact shape of the triangle in the same way as 2:1 described the shape of the Professor's picture. The reason that the 3:4:5 shape is famous is because any triangle with its sides in this ratio has a right angle opposite the longest side. Let's have a look at one. Here's a 3:4:5 triangle that has sides measuring 3 mm, 4 mm and 5 mm.

As you can see, the angle opposite the 5 mm side is exactly 90°. If you don't believe it, you can measure it.

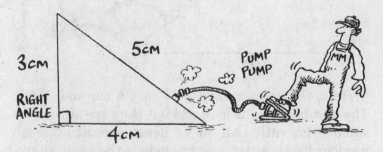

Really? Well, we can soon fix that...

There we are. Now we've pumped it up so that the triangle sides measure 30 mm, 40 mm and 50 mm, which is the same as 3 cm, 4 cm and 5 cm.

Even though each side is 10 times longer than it was before, the ratio of the sides is still 3:4:5. If the ratio of the sides is the same, then the triangle will be exactly the same shape and it will have exactly the same three angles. If you have two or more triangles with the same shape, they are called **similar triangles**.

---

**Similar triangles**
If two or more triangles are *similar* then they always
● have the same three angle measurements
● have their sides in the same ratio.
Even though they can be completely different sizes, they are exactly the same shape.

---

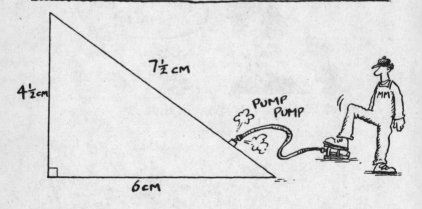

Here, the sides measure $4\frac{1}{2}$ cm , 6 cm and $7\frac{1}{2}$ cm. The numbers might look odd but they are still in the same 3:4:5 ratio. All we've done is multiply each number by $1\frac{1}{2}$. Again, the triangle is the same shape, so it will be similar to the others and will have the same three angles. In fact, we can multiply the sides by any number we like. How about 217?

Sadly, the book isn't quite big enough to fit this triangle in, but if you could see it you'd realize that it is also similar to the other 3:4:5 triangles and that the angles are still exactly the same. Let's just make it a teeny bit bigger still...

Oh. We hadn't finished with 3:4:5 triangles so that's a pity. Never mind, if it blasted Professor Fiendish out of the book then at least it wasn't wasted. We'll send out for another 3:4:5 triangle and look at it later.

**Ratios for other things**

While we're talking about ratios, we should mention that they don't have to involve lengths. When the Sergeant of the Valiant Vector Warriors makes coffee for Colonel Cancel, he knows he needs to put in 1 spoonful of coffee powder, 2 of sugar and 9 spoonfuls of milk. (If the Sergeant doesn't get the milk exactly right, the Colonel refuses to share the biscuits round and then everybody sulks so much that they simply aren't in the mood for marching round and saluting royalty.)

We can describe the ratio of coffee:sugar:milk as 1:2:9.

When the Colonel's playing golf, he likes to take his Thermos flask, which holds 4 cups of coffee. The Sergeant has to make sure that the mixture of coffee, sugar and milk is exactly the same. The question is, how many spoonfuls of each ingredient does he put in? For 1 cup the ratio is 1:2:9 so for 4 cups he needs to multiply everything by 4. It ends up as 4:8:36 which means that the Thermos needs 4 spoons of coffee, 8 of sugar and 36 of milk.

But one morning the Sergeant sleeps in, and by the time he reaches the Colonel's office the corporal is already making the coffee. The Sergeant panics and decides to hide out in the filing cabinet next to the kettle. While he's hiding (and eating the colonel's secret biscuit supply) he hears the teaspoon used a total of 84 times in the day. How many spoonfuls of sugar have been used in total?

The total number of spoonfuls of coffee + sugar + milk = 84.

For each cup of coffee, the total number of

spoonfuls is $1 + 2 + 9 = 12$. Therefore, the number of cups of coffee made is $\frac{84}{12} = 7$. Each cup of coffee has two spoonfuls of sugar, so the number of spoons of sugar $= 7 \times 2 = 14$.

The next day tragedy strikes. The Sergeant (who normally does the shopping) is nowhere to be seen, and the Corporal finds that there are only 6 spoonfuls of sugar to last the whole day. How much milk will he need?

This time we look at the coffee:sugar:milk ratio (which is 1:2:9) and concentrate on the sugar:milk bit. The ratio of sugar to milk is 2:9. So if 2 sugars need 9 milks and we multiply both numbers by 3 we see that 6 sugars will need 27 milks. The big problem is: what does the Corporal do when the sugar runs out?

# POSH DRAWING

Now you've seen how scales work, it's time to find out what to do with your geom set.

Naturally, some people may wish to use the bits to build an intergalactic assault craft, but for those of us who want real nerve-tingling excitement, we're going to draw some triangles. These aren't just your common three-sided doodles either. These triangles are going to be so dead posh that you'll want to check that your calculator isn't cheating with them. Once you can do posh triangles, you can draw pretty much posh anything. So let's get ready for posh drawing: put on your top hat or your diamond tiara, open a packet of caviar crisps and have the servants retire to their quarters.

To draw a triangle you need to know at least three things. These can be:
● The lengths of all three sides
OR...
● The length of one side and two angles
OR...
● The lengths of two sides and one angle.

The way to draw each of these is slightly different as you'll see in a minute. By the way, what *is* useless is if you're told what the three angles are without knowing any of the side lengths. You wouldn't know if your triangle is supposed to be miles across or fit on a pin head.

**When you know three sides**
*A triangle has corners labelled CAT. Side AT = 4 cm, AC= 3 cm and TC = 2 cm. Your mission is to find what each of the three angles are in degrees.*

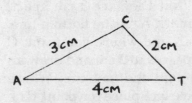

The first thing to do is to make a little rough plan of the triangle. You label the corners C, A and T and then write in the side lengths. This should only take you about 10 seconds, but can save you hours by stopping you going wrong later.

Now we're going to do a version of the triangle that's smart enough to take to the opera. The first thing is to draw the AT side along the bottom and, to be really posh, you do a line *longer than you need*. Then you put your compasses by your ruler, and open them to the exact length you need, which here is 4 cm.

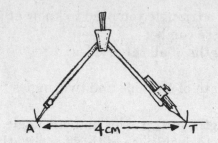

Make a little mark near the end of your line, then stick your compass point on the mark and draw an arc (i.e. small bit of a circle) that goes through the other end of the line. These two marks on the line are where the bottom two corners of the triangle are, so you can mark them A and T.

Now we have a problem. We know the other two lines are 3 cm and 2 cm long but we can't draw them until we know exactly where the top corner "C" of the triangle comes. Here's what to do...

Set your compasses so that they are 3 cm apart, then stick the point in at mark A on the bottom line. Draw an arc somewhere around where you think C will be. Then set your compasses to 2 cm and draw an arc from T that cuts through the last arc. Where these arcs cross over is the exact place for point C.

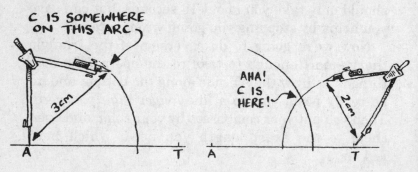

Now you just grab your ruler and draw in two lines to finish the triangle off.

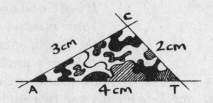

A sign of poshness is to make the lines stick out past the end of the triangle. This also makes life easier if you later need to join some more triangles on or if you need to measure the angles. You can always use a heavier line to make the triangle stand out if you like. Or if you're an arty type, like *some* people we know who have no respect for the sanctity of pure construction, you'll fill up the triangle with the same pattern that's on the vest you're wearing.

Finally, you can measure the angles using the protractor. If you've done a really neat job, you should find they are: C = 104°, A = 29°, T = 47°. They should add up to 180°. If you're a few degrees out, that's still not bad, so don't worry too much.

One person who we *are* worried about is our murderous artist the Evil Reeve. When he drew this triangle his answers were:
C = 104·477512185929923878771034799913°
A = 28·955024371859847757542069598825°
T = 46·567463442210228363686895602620°

...and yes they DO add up to 180°. Isn't that irritating?

## When you know one side and two angles

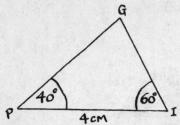

*Draw a triangle PIG with PI = 4 cm, angle P = 40° and angle I = 60°. Your mission is to find the length of side PG.*

Here's another rough diagram, which has a triangle with one side length and two angles marked. First you draw the line PI and put on two marks 4 cm apart to show where the corners of the triangle will be. Now we need to draw in angles of 60° and 40° so, big excitement, you get your protractor out.

To mark out the 60° angle, put your protractor's hot point exactly over point I and make sure the bottom line of the protractor runs along the line PI. Put a mark on the paper where the 60 is on the protractor – and make sure you get the right one! An angle of 60° is acute, so make sure your triangle angle is acute too.

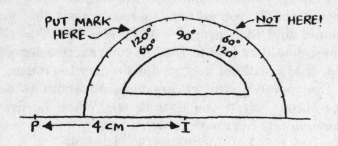

Draw a line going through the new mark and I, and there's your 60° angle. Now draw in the angle of 40° at point P, and it will chop through the last line you drew to complete the triangle.

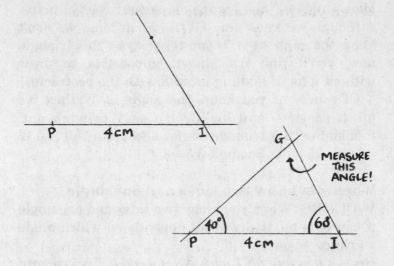

You can test how well you've drawn your angles by measuring the angle G at the top of the triangle. The angles in a triangle always add up to 180°. As we know that the two angles at the bottom are 60° and 40°, this means that G should be 180° − 60° − 40° = 80°.

If you measure the length PG extremely carefully, you should find it's about 3·5 cm. (The Evil Reeve says it should be closer to 3·517540966287267 cm. We don't think he's getting any daylight or eating enough vegetables.)

By the way, here's a little trap to watch out for...

*Draw a triangle COW so OW = 5 cm, angle C = 40° and angle 0 = 75°*

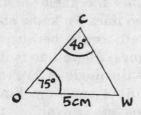

Here's where the rough diagram really helps. Although we know line OW is 5 cm long, we don't know the angle at W. If you try to draw this triangle now, you'll find it's almost impossible to draw without a lot of fiddling around with the protractor!

Of course, if you know the angle at W then it's much easier – and luckily it's easy to work out. Remember that triangle angles add up to 180°, so W = 180 – 75 – 40. So angle W = 65°.

## When you know two sides and one angle

WARNING! When you know two sides and one angle it can be a bit tricky. It all depends on which angle you know about.

*Draw a triangle ANT with AN = 4 cm, NT = 5 cm and angle N = 110°.*

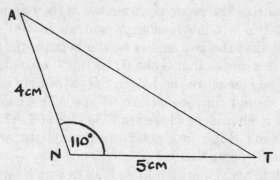

This is easy to draw because the angle we know about comes between the two lines we know about. This is called the **included angle** because it's included between the two lines. All you do is draw line NT 5 cm long, measure the angle of 110° at N and then draw your AN line 4 cm long. Finally connect A and T and there you are. Hurrah.

The problems come when the one angle you're given is *not* the included angle! (An angle that isn't included is called an **excluded** angle.)

*Draw a triangle DOG with OG = 5 cm DO = 3 cm and angle G = 30°.*

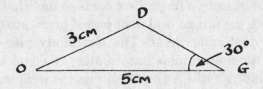

First you draw OG 5 cm long. That's easy.

Next you measure an angle of 30° at point G and draw a line. You know point D will be somewhere on this line. The question is – where?

Finally you open your compasses to 3 cm, stick them in at O and draw an arc to cut the last line you drew...

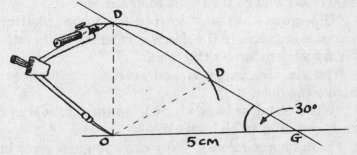

...but it cuts the line in *two* places! Either one could be point D, because both of them are 3 cm from O and both of them are on an angle of 30° from G. Weird or what? Mind you, very occasionally confusing measurements like this do have their uses. Why not grab your compasses, a ruler and a big bit of paper and see if you can solve:

45

**The Mystery of Bluetooth's Buried Bullion**
City:     Chicago, Illinois, USA
Place:   Luigi's Diner, Upper Main St
Date:    15 January 1930
Time:   5:30 pm

The door of Luigi's diner flew open so fast that sparks shot from the hinges and it slammed back into the wall with a deafening BAM! The six shady men sitting around the central table immediately dived underneath it, grabbing anything they could use as weapons.

"You'll never take us alive!" shouted Blade Bocelli from between the chair legs. Crammed in behind him were Porky, Half-Smile, Weasel, Numbers and One Finger Jimmy.

"Yeah," snarled Weasel, trying to look tough. "I've got a teaspoon and I'm not afraid to use it."

"He means it!" said Half-Smile Gabrianni. "One step closer and he'll stir you to death."

"Hey, guys – it's me!" gasped Chainsaw Charlie, who was standing in the doorway catching his breath. "What ya doin' under the table?"

The six men groaned and started crawling out across the floor.

"When the door banged open, we thought it was a raid, you numbskull," said Weasel.

"Yeah," agreed Porky. "Why can't you just come in quietly like other folks?"

"Sorry," said Chainsaw as he pulled up a chair and sat down. "But you'll never guess who I just saw!"

"We don't care," said Jimmy crossly, brushing old bits of dusty pasta off his trousers.

"I think you do care," said Chainsaw. "I saw Bluetooth Fonetti."

"BLUETOOTH FONETTI?" cried the others.

"He's been dead six months!" said Weasel. "I remember it. He died just after he raided that gold bullion from the Fort Knocks vaults."

"Never found that bullion, did they?" said Jimmy.

"Maybe not, but I found Bluetooth," said Chainsaw. "And he looks pretty good for a dead guy. Wearing a new suit and walking past the Mission House."

"Are you sure it was Bluetooth?" asked Blade.

"Sure I'm sure," said Chainsaw. "I recognized him by his blue tooth. Funny thing, though. I called his name and off he shot like a tiger was eating him."

"If a tiger was eating him he wouldn't be able to run," said Numbers. "You mean like a tiger was running after him."

"Eating, running – it's all the same," said Chainsaw.

"No, it ain't!" sniggered Weasel. He pointed at Porky who was already calming his nerves with a couple of roast chickens and a bucketful of spaghetti. "If  Porky could run as well as he can eat he'd be like an express train in pants."

"Whatever," said Chainsaw. "It was Bluetooth and I called his name and off he ran. So what d'ya say to that?"

"I say we go and find him," said Blade. "I want to ask him how he came alive again."

"Oh no you don't," said a sharp voice from the private booth behind them.

A set of painted fingernails reached through the curtain that hung across the booth and tugged it open. A waft of expensive perfume floated towards them.

"Dolly Snowlips!" gasped Blade. "How long have you been there?"

"Long enough to recognize a fool when I see one," said Dolly Snowlips. "Can't you put two and two together?"

"I didn't see any twos!" protested Blade, but Dolly wasn't listening.

Dolly rose to her feet and clicked her high heels across the floor towards the windows. She pulled down the blinds and flicked off the switch for the outside lights. Turning back, she noticed Benni the waiter waiting nervously by the counter.

"Relax, Benni," she said. "You just closed early tonight."

Dolly joined the others at the table and spoke in a hushed voice. "I don't want you guys telling anyone that Bluetooth's up and around, understand?"

"Why not?" they replied.

"Oh, brother!" She sighed. "It's so simple I thought even you mugs might get it. Listen: when Bluetooth grabbed the gold, he couldn't just go and spend it. He had to disappear for a while and, in the meantime, he had to make sure the gold was safe somewhere. So, first of all, he tells everyone that he's dead. . ."

"How can you tell anyone you're dead?" demanded Chainsaw. "They ain't gonna believe you. They'll see your mouth moving when you're telling them."

"He didn't actually tell them! He just fixed up his own funeral and word got out."

"That's smart," murmured the men.

"Here's the *really* smart bit," continued Dolly. "When they buried the coffin out in the middle of the old prairie, it wasn't him inside. It was the gold. A nice little service all official with the preacher and everything. All that bullion was stashed away and nobody suspected a thing. And, by the way, I look fabulous in a black veil."

"You mean you were there?" gasped Blade.

"Of course I was there," snapped Dolly. "Who d'ya think thought of the whole scheme?"

"So you know where Bluetooth's coffin is?" said Weasel. "A coffin full of gold?"

"Of course I know," said Dolly.

"So where is it?" demanded Blade. "We could use some of that."

"Oh, yeah," sneered Dolly. "Like I'm gonna tell you punks!"

Blade pulled his nasty face.

"Look here, Dolly. You and us work as a team so what we got we share. That gold in the coffin is ours as well as yours."

"In your dreams," said Dolly. "I'm on a different team now, the me-and-Bluetooth team. So that gold belongs to me and Bluetooth."

"I thought the gold belonged to the fort," said Numbers.

"Don't start getting technical!" snapped Dolly. "The fact is you guys ain't getting it."

"Oh, really," said Blade. "And what if we put the

word out that Bluetooth was up and around? What if the fort officials came asking you a few questions, Dolly? What then, eh?"

"You wouldn't dare," said Dolly uncertainly.

"Oh, no?" said Blade. "You tell us where that coffin is or we go and talk to the fort."

With a sigh, Dolly rose to her feet and went over to the wall where a few dusty pictures of Luigi's regular customers hung. She took down a faded print and brought it over to the table. Written across the bottom were the words: *Mr EB Fonetti RIP*. When she turned it over, they saw writing on the back.

The Last Resting Place of Bluetooth Fonetti

• The Singing Cactus is 50 paces from Skull Rock.
• Skull Rock is 65 paces from Red Water Well.
• The Well is 20 paces from the Singing Cactus.
• Bluetooth, the cactus and the well all lie in a straight line. Bluetooth is buried exactly 45 paces from Skull Rock.

"Is this right?" demanded Blade.

"Sure is," smiled Dolly slipping back into the booth. "But that's all I'm telling you. Now, if you don't mind, I've got an urgent appointment with a chocolate ice."

"You think we're so completely dumb that we can't work this out, don't you?" said Blade.

"Oh, you're not completely dumb," said Dolly. "After

all, you're smart enough to work out what I think of you."

"Er ..." began Chainsaw, "... so does that mean we're dumb or that we're smart? If I've got this right, she says we're smart enough to work out that she thinks we're dumb. And we must have worked it out right because she said we were smart enough to see that she thinks we're dumb, which means we've gotta be dumb or what we worked out wouldn't have been right. Right?"

But Blade wasn't listening. Instead, he cleared everything off the table with a sweep of his arm.

"C'mon guys," he chuckled. "We'll show her. We're going to make a map right here on the table."

"But how do we do the measurements?" asked Porky.

"Simple," said Blade. "We'll mark them out with breadsticks. Each breadstick is the same as 10 paces."

"So half a bread stick is 5 paces" said Numbers. "So 65 paces is the same as six and a half breadsticks."

"Er ... yeah!" said Blade. "I was going to say that."

"But if we'd been dumb," persisted Chainsaw, "and still managed to work out that we were dumb, then that would have been pretty smart, right? But then we wouldn't have been dumb so we would have worked it out wrong, so that would have been dumb."

"Enough!" snapped Blade. "Now, let's get to work."

And so with breadsticks, the mustard jar, a pepper grinder, a coffee cup and a vase of flowers they made a map of the Old Prairie on the table.

"Lookin' good so far," said Blade, once the vase, the peppermill and the coffee cup were in position. "All we need to do is find the spot that's in line with the

51

coffee cup and the vase, and is also four and a half breadsticks from the pepper grinder."

"I got it!" said Numbers, carefully arranging the last breadsticks. "Look – the mustard jar marks the exact spot."

"Wow!" they gasped.

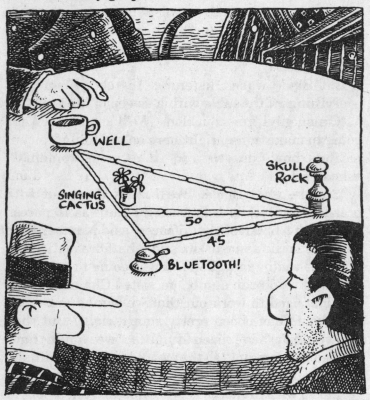

"So that means Bluetooth's gold is in the mustard jar," said Blade.

The other men immediately all tried to grab the jar at once.

"No, you dummies!" said Blade. "This is just the

plan. Now all we need to do is measure how far the mustard jar is from the vase."

"I make it almost exactly one breadstick," said Numbers.

"So that means the gold is about ten paces away from the cactus in line with the well," said Blade. He called over to Dolly who had gone back to the private booth.

"We've got it, Dolly!" He laughed. "That surprised you, didn't it? You can't still be thinking we're dumb now."

Dolly Snowlips said nothing. Instead, she just gave Blade a cold stare.

"The thing is," said Chainsaw, "a dumb guy can't say he's dumb because that's smart, so he wouldn't be dumb after all. And a smart guy can't say he's dumb because he'd be wrong so he wouldn't be smart. But if a dumb guy says he's smart, that makes sense because he'd be wrong which is dumb which is what he is, and a smart guy who says he's smart is fine too, because he'd be right. So no matter if you're smart or dumb you've got to say you're smart."

"That's it, Chainsaw!" grinned Blade. "Whatever way you look at it, I'm smart! Jimmy, go and get some shovels from the cemetery. The rest of you, very carefully carry the table outside with the stuff laid out on it, and get it into the automobile. We're going to dig up that coffin!"

Together they scrambled through the door with the table and, seconds later, a car engine started up in the street. Benni the waiter approached Dolly, who was left sitting alone clutching her bowl of chocolate ice cream.

"Say Miss Snowlips," he said. "You've not touched your ice and it's all melted. I guess you're worried they'll get all the gold?"

"Not really." Dolly glanced at Benni and smiled coolly. In fact she was so cool that when she blew on her chocolate ice it immediately froze over again.

"So didn't you give them right directions?"

"Sure I did," said Dolly. "What d'ya take me for? A liar? Those are the right directions to the gold, but trust me, all those saps are gonna get is a load of blisters!"

* * *

Can you see why Blade and the gang will be digging in the wrong place?

To solve this properly, we'll make a scale drawing. You can get a rough idea of how it will turn out by looking back at Blade's map with the breadsticks. We'll use a scale of 1 mm = 1 pace, and first we'll draw the triangle that links the well, the cactus and the rock. The first part of the directions tell us:

> • The Singing Cactus is 50 paces from Skull Rock.
> • Skull Rock is 65 paces from Red Water Well.
> • The Well is 20 paces from the Singing Cactus.

This is a triangle where we know the lengths of all three sides. To start with we'll draw a line CR that's 50 mm long. This represents the distance from the cactus to the rock. Next we need to find where the well is so we use compasses to draw an arc 20 mm from point C. Finally we draw an arc 65 mm from point R. Where the two arcs cross is where the well is...

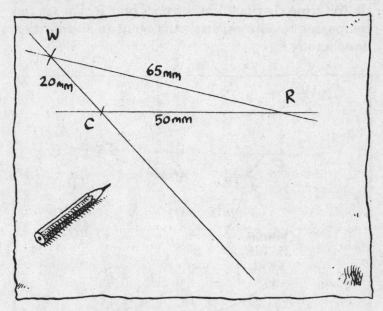

We've extended the line WC because we know Bluetooth's coffin is somewhere along it. Let's see what the directions say:

> • Bluetooth, the cactus and the well all lie in a straight line. Bluetooth is buried exactly 45 paces from Skull Rock.

We're about to make a second triangle, joining the points CRB where B is Bluetooth's coffin. So far, we've got the length of one side CR, and we also have the angle at point C. We don't know what the angle is in degrees, but that doesn't matter because the CWR triangle has shown us exactly which direction the line to B points. All we need to do now is find a place on the WC line that is 45 mm from point R. We set the compasses to 45 mm, stick the point in R and then draw an arc.

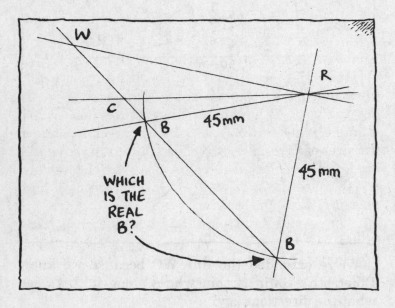

Good grief. The arc cuts the line in *two* places, both marked B!

This is why the directions have been so sneaky. They have described a triangle giving two sides and an *excluded* angle. Blade thought he'd found the third point of the triangle but he never realized there were two places where the coffin might be buried!

# THE TRICKS OF TRIG

Aha! Just in time, our replacement 3:4:5 triangle has arrived fresh from the factory. While it's being unwrapped, we'll explain the little challenge we've got for you. Although we know the sides of the triangle are in the ratio 3:4:5, we don't know the sizes of the angles, so can you find out how big the angles are as accurately as possible? Obviously the simplest way is to grab your protractor and measure them and we'll give you a clue to start you off: the square-ish-looking right angle measures exactly 90°. (By the way, sorry about the bump in the triangle. Obviously when this triangle was being put together in the Murderous Maths factory, something sneaked inside. If you see it wriggle just give it a thump.) You should find that one of the other angles measures a bit more than 50° and the other measures a bit less than 40°.

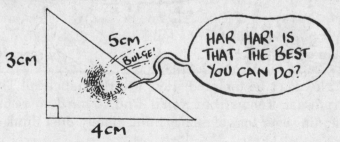

3cm

5cm
BULGE!

4cm

HAR HAR! IS THAT THE BEST YOU CAN DO?

Good grief! We're getting cheek from a talking triangle. (What's more, if you put your nose too close it seems to have a mouldy Brussel-sprout smell. How ghastly.) Oh, well. If the triangle is going to be fussy, look at your protractor carefully and you'll see that the angles are about 53° and about 37°. How's that?

Oh, no! It's Professor Fiendish. We thought he'd got blown out of the book back on page 35. He must have sneaked into the triangle factory with his pet pig and they've been camping inside the new 3:4:5 triangle ever since it was assembled. Whatever you do, be cool.

No, don't be tempted! How utterly diabolical! The Professor knows that you'll find it hard to resist handing over tons of money immediately. Just think of the admiring glances you'll get when you open your geometry set and pull out a mechanized protractor the size of an armchair. It's tough, but try not to drool at the thought of measuring angles such as 73·459°.

YOU KNOW YOU WANT ONE!

No, we don't. Besides there's a way we can find out what the angles in this triangle are that's accurate to 0·000001° or even better. We don't use a protractor, we use *trigonometry*.

## What does trigonometry do?
If you've got a right-angled triangle, you only need to know the lengths of two sides, or one side and one of the smaller angles, and you can work out everything else. Here's all you need to know:

$$\sin = \frac{\text{opposite}}{\text{hypotenuse}} \quad \text{or} \quad S = \frac{O}{H}$$

$$\cos = \frac{\text{adjacent}}{\text{hypotenuse}} \quad \text{or} \quad C = \frac{A}{H}$$

$$\tan = \frac{\text{opposite}}{\text{adjacent}} \quad \text{or} \quad T = \frac{O}{A}$$

(triangle labelled: hypotenuse, opposite, adjacent)

Got that? No? Well, don't worry. If you've never seen a hypotenuse or sin, cos and tan before, go and sit yourself on the shaded angle of the triangle and you'll soon see how it works.

The longest side of the right-angled triangle is called the **hypotenuse.** The side opposite you is called the **opposite** and the other side is called the **adjacent**. ("Adjacent" is a fancy word that means "next" because the side is next to you.)

**UGLY NUMBER WARNING**
**We're about to produce some really fancy long decimal fractions, but to stop them getting out of control and taking over the planet, most of them will be rounded off to 2, 3 or 4 digits depending on what mood we're in. However, occasionally we'll show some fractions with LOADS of digits just for the sheer fun of it.**

### The secrets of sin

Let's suppose you know the length of the *opposite* side and also the length of the *hypotenuse* of your right-angled triangle. If you divide the opposite length by the hypotenuse length you get a special fraction called the **sin** (see page 72) of the angle you're sitting on. (You pronounce this as SINE, so that people don't think you're talking about the horribly evil sort of sin such as not putting the top back on the toothpaste or teaching your parrot to make burpy noises.) Most people remember the sin formula with just three letters: $\mathbf{S} = \frac{O}{H}$. You can convert this fraction into a measurement in degrees, and that way you can find out how big your angle is.

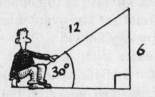

For instance, if the opposite side was 6 and the hypotenuse was 12, when you work out $\frac{O}{H}$ you get 6 ÷ 12 = 0·5. You can then convert this fraction to find out that your angle is 30°. (You'll see how to do these conversions in the next chapter.) This result is written like this: sin30° = 0·5.

It doesn't matter how big or small your triangle is. The only thing that affects the size of an angle is the ratio of the sides. Have a look at these similar triangles:

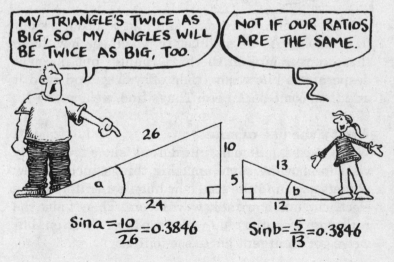

Both these right-angled triangles have sides in the ratio of 5:12:13, but one is twice as big as the other. In the bigger triangle, if we want to work out the sin of angle $a$ we put the length of the opposite side (which is 10) over the length of the hypotenuse (which is 26). We get get $\sin a = \frac{10}{26} = 0\cdot3846$.

If we do the same thing with the smaller triangle we get $\sin b = \frac{5}{13} = 0\cdot3846$. Even though the triangles are different sizes, $\sin a$ and $\sin b$ both equal $0\cdot3846$ which means that the angles $a$ and $b$ are the same size.

(Just out of interest, angles $a$ and $b$ both work out to be $22\cdot62°$. As we said before, you'll see how to do these conversions in the next chapter but if you're desperate to know now, then off you go and read it and then come back here. That's fine, we'll wait.)

## What's the use of sines?
When maths gets more murderous, sines are utterly vital in showing some amazing things such as how planets go round the sun, how huge generators make electricity and how radio waves work. There's also the rather groovy sine rule which we'll see later on, but we've got an urgent job to see to first…

> Dear Murderous Maths,
> Our house needs a slide from the
> bedroom window down to the garden.
> Could you tell us how high up
> the wall it would come?

Whoever wrote this must be a bit mad because even though the answer will involve sines, they forgot to "sign" it. However, they did put in a rough plan:

Strange-looking place, but so long as the wall goes up at a right angle, working out the height of the top of the slide should be easy enough. The length of the slide is 7 m and the angle of the slide is going to be 40°, which is about perfect for a nice fast ride without banging your bottom too hard when you hit the ground at the end.

Let's start by drawing a triangle like this:

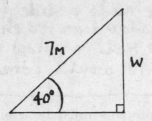

Our triangle has a hypotenuse that measures 7 m, and if we call the height up the wall $w$ we know this is opposite the angle of 40°.

Using the sin formula, $\sin = \frac{O}{H}$, we get:

$\sin 40° = \frac{w}{7}$

So far so good, but how do you find out what $w$ is? If you've read *The Phantom X* (available in all good bookshops and some pretty grotty bookshops too) then you'll already know enough about algebra to work out $w$. If you haven't read it, then don't worry. All we need to do is shuffle the bits of the equation round so that we have the $w$ on one side and the numbers on the other. This is rather neat so stand well back and pay close attention...

If we multiply both sides of the equation by 7 we get:

$7 \times \sin 40° = 7 \times \frac{w}{7}$

On the right-hand side the $w$ is being multiplied *and* divided by 7, so they cancel out, and you just get $w$.

Therefore we end up with:

$7 \times \sin 40° = w$

To make it neater you can swap the sides over to get:

$w = 7 \times \sin 40°$

Now you're a bit stuck because you need to know what $\sin 40°$ is and you can't work it out until you've read the next chapter. However, because we love you (and we've already read the next chapter), we'll tell you that sin40° = 0·643. Actually it's more like 0·64278761 but 3 decimal places is enough for now. Good grief, we're only fixing up a slide, we're not designing a space station.

So now we have:

$$w = 7 \times 0\cdot643$$

and when you work it out you get:

$$w = 4\cdot501$$

This is about the only bit of algebra you need in trig, but we'll be using it a lot. You might want to fold over the corner of this page, so you can quickly turn back and find how it works again later on. In the meantime, we can knock on the door and tell whoever's inside that the slide meets the wall at a height of 4·501 metres.

Huh, we might have known. It's the utterly nutty Pure Mathematicians' house. Who else would have a slide down from the bedroom window? Anyway, the next thing is to see how far away from the house the slide touches the ground. We'd better make sure it doesn't go into the duck pond.

Here's the triangle:

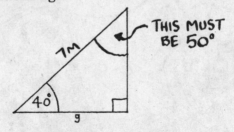

THIS MUST BE 50°

7M

40°

g

What we *could* do is work out the top angle of the triangle. As all the angles in a triangle add up to 180°, the top angle must be 180° − 90° − 40° = 50°. The side opposite the 50° angle is $g$ and the hypotenuse is still 7, so we'd get $\sin 50° = \frac{g}{7}$, and then we could work that out... BUT we've already done a bit of sin so let's have a refreshing change.

## Time to try cos

Cos does a very similar job to sin, but instead of making a fraction using the opposite side and the hypotenuse, cos = $\frac{\text{adjacent}}{\text{hypotenuse}}$ or $C = \frac{A}{H}$. This is rather handy right now because if you look at our little triangle, you'll see that the angle we know is 40°, the hypotenuse is still 7 m and the distance along the ground $g$ is the adjacent side. We can write $\cos 40° = \frac{g}{7}$ and using the same bit of algebra as before, we can turn it into $g = 7 \times \cos 40°$.

Cos values are not the same as sin values, so once again we'll give you a sneak preview of the next chapter and tell you that $\cos 40° = 0.766$. If we put that in we get $g = 7 \times 0.766 = 5.362$. Therefore the bottom of the slide will reach the ground 5.362 metres from the house.

## The Pythagoras test

If you don't quite trust this trigonometric wizardry, we can call on the ancient Greek mathematician Pythagoras to check our answers with his famous theorem.

$$a^2 + b^2 = c^2$$

THIS WORKS FOR ANY RIGHT-ANGLED TRIANGLE!

Pythagoras' theorem says that if you square the lengths of the two smaller sides and add them together, that must equal the square of the hypotenuse.

Here are the results of our slide calculations:

Therefore we need to check that $(5.362)^2 + (4.501)^2 = 7^2$.

If we work out the left-hand side we get: $28.751 + 20.259$ and that comes to $49.01$. On the right-hand side we have $7^2 = 49$, so as you can see the answers are extremely close. If we had used the exact values of sin40° and cos40° instead of having them rounded off to three decimal places, the answers would have been exactly the same. In other words … TRIGONOMETRY WORKS!

### Are right-angled triangles really worth all this fuss?

Yes they are, actually. One reason is that if you make sandwiches with sliced bread and chop them diagonally, you get right-angled triangles and for some reason they always taste better. Another reason is that almost any calculation involving distance or directions will end up using a right-angled triangle. One of the most common examples is when you need to measure the height of something big. Usually the best way of doing this involves using tan.

## How to measure the height of a marauding giant with tan

If you see a giant marauding around the countryside squashing trees and eating cows, it makes sense to check that he's not breaking any local by-laws regarding height. Tell him to stand still on some flat place – you may need to speak quite sternly because giants can get moody when their marauding is interrupted. Once he's in position, go and stand some distance back from him. Let's say you're 15 metres away. Next, you need to measure the "angle of elevation" to the top of his head.

This diagram shows what we mean:

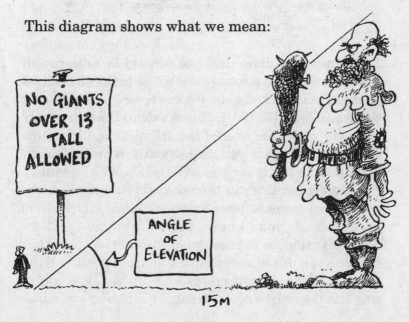

NO GIANTS OVER 13 TALL ALLOWED

ANGLE OF ELEVATION

15M

One way to measure angles involving big things is to get three long thin sticks and make them into a triangle held by elastic bands. Lay one stick on the ground pointing at the giant's feet, and then adjust the triangle so that one of the other sticks points exactly towards the top of his head.

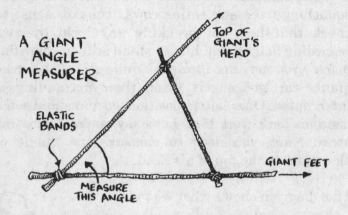

A GIANT
ANGLE
MEASURER

TOP OF
GIANT'S
HEAD

ELASTIC
BANDS

GIANT FEET

MEASURE
THIS ANGLE

When you've done this, you should be able to use your protractor to measure the angle between the two sticks. If you wanted to be really clever you'd measure the exact lengths of the three sticks then draw an accurate scale diagram of the triangle and measure the angle off it. (Or you could even call on Cosgirl to work out the angle for you with the "cosine formula". You'll meet her later in the book.)

Anyway, suppose your angle is 40° and you know the adjacent side is 15 m, this makes a nice little right-angled triangle. The opposite side is $h$, which is the height of the giant.

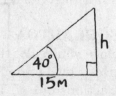

40°

$h$

15m

You'll notice that we're dealing with the adjacent and opposite sides, and that's when it's time to use tan. Tan works in the same way as sin and cos, and if you check the formulas, you'll find that tan $= \frac{\text{opposite}}{\text{adjacent}}$ or $\mathbf{T} = \frac{\mathbf{O}}{\mathbf{A}}$. Here, the opposite side is $h$ (the height of the giant), the adjacent side is 15 and the angle is 40° so we can put $\tan 40° = \frac{h}{15}$.

This adjusts to:

$$h = 15 \times \tan 40°$$

All we need to know now is the value of tan40°, which is 0·839. Guess how we knew that? Answer: because we've read the next chapter.

Therefore $h = 15 \times 0·839 = 12·585$.

As the giant is 12·585 m tall, you can give him the good news that he doesn't exceed the 13 m limit, which means that you're not going to march him briskly along to the nearest police station. You can let him stomp off and get his marauding finished.

(By the way, this method of working out heights also works for tall buildings. All you need to do is find a block of flats that is marauding around the countryside squashing trees and eating cows, and tell it to stand still on some flat place. . .)

## SOHCAHTOA

Once you've got the hang of sin, cos and tan, the only tricky bit is remembering which sides to make your fractions out of. This is where SOHCAHTOA comes in. It's a squished-up version of $S = \frac{O}{H}$, $C = \frac{A}{H}$ and $T = \frac{O}{A}$. There are all sorts of silly ways to help you remember this. You can either practise saying it like "soak-are-toe-er" (which makes it sound like a strange old volcano) or you make up a silly sentence starting each word with the letters from SOHCAHTOA like this:

*Summer On Holiday, Christmas At Home, Teacher's Off Anyway.*

**Where did the names sin, cos and tan come from?**
Just to clear things up, sin, cos and tan are all nicknames. The real names for these bits are SINE, COSINE and TANGENT. Although people still say "SINE", they usually write it as sin. You may wonder why anybody thought it was worth knocking the "E" off but there's a very good reason. If we replaced every "SIN" in this book with "SINE", we'd need an extra 197 letter Es. Then if we print 100,000 copies of the book, that would be an extra 19,700,000 Es. That's enough Es to fill about 141 more books. Imagine 141 books just full of the letter E. Boring or what?

If you think knocking the E off SINE is silly, wait until you hear where the name "sine" comes from. It comes from the Latin word "sinus" which means a bay. Yes, that's right. *Bay* as in big curved bit of the coastline by the seaside with little boats sailing across it full of people eating ice cream. Go on, then. See if you can work out the connection between these two:

$Sin =$

$opposite/$ $hypotenuse$

Give in?

The whole idea of sines started in ancient India and then about 1,200 years ago they were developed by a brilliant Arab mathematician living in Baghdad.

He was called Al-Khorezmi and he was the first person to set down a proper table of values for sines. (Incidentally, he was also the first person to call algebra *algebra*.) He used the Indian name for sines, but by the time he'd copied it from Indian into Arabic it appeared as something like "jb".

Over 200 years later, the Spanish King Alphonso VI raided the Arab library which held Al-Khorezmi's stuff and had it translated into Latin. One of the translators found the word "jb" and didn't realize it was supposed to be Indian. Instead he thought it was an Arabic word. The closest word in Arabic he could find to "jb" meant "bay" and so he translated it into the latin word for bay – sinus.

So there you are. Obvious when you think about it, isn't it?

Now then, it's time for something rather special. You've been told about it, you've been promised that it's coming, you've waited patiently and by jingo you jolly well deserve it, so take a deep breath as we proudly present you with...

Er, no. It's the *next chapter*...

# THE FORBIDDEN BUTTONS

Who needs to measure them when we can work them out? If you look at the triangle, the two unknown angles are marked *s* and *l*. (This stands for the *smaller* angle and the *larger* angle.) We can work out what these angles are by using sin. First of all we can quickly see that $\sin s = \frac{3}{5} = 0\cdot6$ and we can see that $\sin l = \frac{4}{5} = 0\cdot8$. All we need to do now is to convert these fractions into degrees.

Sorry, Professor, but if you can only measure to the nearest 0·1 of a degree, that's no good for true Murderous Maths fans.

In the olden days, people had to do conversions by studying massive bits of paper covered in tables of tiny numbers, but luckily we've got a much easier way of doing it now. Prepare yourself for a shock though, because this is one of those very rare times in a Murderous Maths book when we have to swallow our pride and ... *reach for a calculator!*

### Testing the forbidden buttons on your calculator

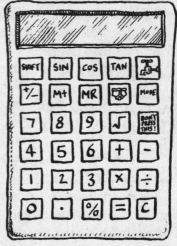

Have you got one of those calculators that has loads of mysterious extra buttons that you've never dared touch yet?

The buttons we're going to play with are sin, cos, tan and SHIFT.

Some calculators have INV or even "2nd FCN" instead of SHIFT but don't worry because they all do pretty much the same thing. Whatever your button's called, from now in this book we'll just call it SHIFT.

If you haven't got a calculator with these buttons on but you're allowed to use a computer, find the computer's calculator. (Look in programmes/accessories.) Once you've found it, under the "view" option choose "scientific".

**If you haven't got a fancy calculator, then don't worry. We'll give you all the answers anyway so you'll still be able to see what's going on.**

You now need to find out what sort of calculator you've got because there are three different types that do sin/cos/tan sums.

**What sort of calculator have you got?**

| | |
|---|---|
| Old-fashioned: | These usually just have one big row of digits on the screen. |
| Modern or "dual": | These have a big row of digits for the answer and then above that there is a second smaller row of digits that shows you which buttons you've just pushed. |
| Calcatronic Hawk: | No screen and no buttons. You just point the calculator at whatever sum you want doing and then it uses an |

The answer is beyond your feeble human understanding.

electro-kinetic photon drive to levitate the nearest pencil and write the answer neatly on the paper for you. All very clever but where's the fun? It's a bit like watching somebody playing a video game without letting you have a go. No wonder they haven't really caught on and you don't see them in the shops.

Most people these days have the modern sort of calculator, so all the instructions coming up are for them. However, if your calculator is old-fashioned (and that includes most computer calculators) you need to press the buttons in a slightly different order. Read through the next bit and then see the special message in the box.

## Making angles into fractions

First of all we'll test the sin button to make sure it hasn't gone mouldy. Wipe off any cobwebs and then press the cancel or AC button to clear all the dead numbers out. Ready? We'll start by checking the value you get for sin30°.

- Press *sin 30* = (Of course you can't put in the little degree sign ° but don't worry. The calculator will guess that you mean degrees. Oooh, they're so clever.)
- The answer should be 0·5.

DON'T BE OLD-FASHIONED! TREAT YOURSELF TO THE FIENDISH ANGLETRON!

## Calculator sabotage!

If you get a completely strange answer then don't worry. Your calculator hasn't blown a fuse or run out of petrol or anything. What's usually happened is that some evil person has sabotaged it by playing with the MODE button.

If your answer is − 0·9880 then you'll probably

HAR HAR! SERVES YOU RIGHT! BUT THE ANGLETRON IS TOTALLY SABOTAGE-PROOF!

THAT'S BECAUSE THE 'MODE' BUTTON DOESN'T WORK...

notice on the screen somewhere in tiny letters it says "RAD" or just the letter "R" which means the calculator is in "radians" mode. If your calculator says 0·45399 then it's in "grads" mode which is even more useless. If you've read *Desperate Measures* you'll know what radians and grads are, and you'll also know that we don't want them coming anywhere near us, so you need to put the calculator into "degrees" mode. On a modern calculator, you usually do this by pushing the button marked "MODE" a few times until the word "DEG" comes up on the screen, then push the number 1. Now try pressing *sin 30* = and hope you get 0·5. If that doesn't work, then you're in big big trouble, because you'll have to admit defeat and go and find the instructions. Good luck.

Once you've got sin 30 working, try the cos and tan buttons:

● Press *cos 60* = and the answer should be 0·5.

● Press *tan 45* = and the answer should be 1.

How are you doing? Once you've got these sums to work, then you can get the sin or cos or tan of any angles you like. But be warned. Most answers involve long decimals that will fill the screen.

**What to look for when you're messing around**
There are all sorts of quaint and curious little things to look out for when you mess around with the sin, cos and tan buttons. Here are a few of them for you to experiment with. (We won't bother with the explanations of how and why they happen right now because we deal with it all later on. This is just PLAYTIME so have fun.)

● You'll find that with sin or cos you can't get answers that are bigger than 1, but you can with tan.

● If you play with the sin button for a while, you'll find that as the angles get closer to 90°, the answers get nearer and nearer to 1. But then if you're feeling a bit crazy, you could try working out sin91° and you should find that you get the same answer as sin89°. And if you try sin92° you'll get the same answer as sin88°. And if you try sin93° …well, you work it out. If you *really* want to go mad try getting an answer for sin179°. You get the same answer as 1°. Now, if you try sin181° you'll get what looks like the same answer again but with a very tiny difference. Can you spot it?

> A minus sign appears in front of the sin of any angle between 180° and 360°.

(We'll find out more about what happens with angles bigger than 90° later on using a bucket of paint and a tow truck.)

- **sin $x$ = cos (90 – $x$)**

This means that if you have two angles that add up to 90°, then the sin of one will equal the cos of the other. For instance sin25° = cos65° = 0·422618261.

- **tan $x$ = $\dfrac{\sin x}{\cos x}$**

If you know the sin of an angle and the cos of an angle you can work out the tan because tan = $\frac{\sin}{\cos}$. If you want to try it, pick any angle you like, such as 38°. Press *sin 38 ÷ cos 38 =* then remember the answer. Now clear the screen then push *tan 38 =*. Does it match?

## Making fractions into angles

So far, we've made angles into fractions, but you can also turn a fraction into an angle by using sin (or cos or tan) backwards. To do this you use the SHIFT button on your calculator (or the INV or 2nd FCN button if that's what you've got). You always press SHIFT immediately before sin, cos or tan, so let's test it:

● Press *SHIFT sin 0·5 =* and the answer should be 30

Old-fashioned calculators: again put the number in first. So if you push *0·5 SHIFT sin* (or *0·5 INV sin)* the answer should be 30.

This is called using the INVERSE of sin, which we can write down as $\sin^{-1}$. If you are one of our most highly intelligent Murderous Maths readers, you will now have realized why the SHIFT button is marked INV on some calculators. By the way, the sum you've just worked out is $\sin^{-1} 0·5 = 30°$.

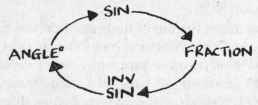

Now try $\cos^{-1}$ and $\tan^{-1}$.

- Press *SHIFT cos 0·5* = and the answer should be 60.
- Press *SHIFT tan 1* = and the answer should be 45. If you've got this far you've done well!

What a sad little man the Professor is. He just doesn't get it, does he? Doesn't he realize that one thousandth of a degree is simply not close enough for true Murderous Maths fans. This is the grand moment we've been waiting for, so let's show him what *real* accuracy is.

We know that sin*s* = 0·6 and as we want to convert the fraction of 0·6 into an angle we'll use sin⁻¹.

- Press *SHIFT sin 0·6 =*
- and you'll see the answer is roughly:
  36·869897645844021296855612559034°

You couldn't get an answer as accurate as that on your sad old Angletron, eh, Professor?

Oh dear, he's getting desperate. Notice how he's rubbed out the "5" so he thinks we won't be able to work out what the angle *l* is! Don't worry, we can use tan⁻¹ instead. Remember $T = \frac{O}{A}$, therefore $\tan l = \frac{4}{3}$. This means that $l = \tan^{-1}\frac{4}{3}$.

Press "cancel" or "AC" then watch this:

- First press *4 ÷ 3 =*
  (Here we've just divided the opposite side of the triangle by the adjacent side. Now we convert the answer into degrees.)
- Press *SHIFT* and then *tan =*

- You'll see the answer is:
  53·13010235415597870314438744409066°

The Professor thinks it's "not right", eh? Well, it's simple enough to check. The angles in a triangle add up to 180°, so if we add up our two answers with the right angle we get:

```
    90
 +  53·13010235415597870314438744409066
 +  36·86989764584402129685561255590934
   ─────────────────────────────────────
 = 180
```

Isn't that fun?

**How to make your calculator blow up**

What happens if you're supposed to push SHIFT sin but you forget to push the SHIFT button? If you're

desperate to know, then you can give it a go, but first put on very thick gloves. Put sin 0·625 into the calculator and then holding the calculator at arm's length, give the = button a quick push. When the smoke has cleared away look at

the screen. Instead of 38·68218745° you'll find that the answer is something useless like 0·010908091.

The reason for this is that when you push SHIFT it tells the calculator that you're about to put in a fraction that you want to turn into degrees. If you *don't* push SHIFT then the calculator thinks you're putting in degrees. So when you put in sin 0·625 and then pushed =, the calculator thought you had a silly little angle of 0·625° which you wanted turning into a fraction. You've just found out that sin0·625° = 0·010908091 so no wonder it got hot and a bit fed up.

If you want to be even more daring you could find out what happens when you push SHIFT by accident. This time you need to wear a suit of armour and have a fire extinguisher handy. You'll also need a long thin stick. First you put in SHIFT sin followed by an angle such as 42° and then stand well back. Use the stick to press = then quickly dive behind the sofa.

If you're lucky, your calculator will have a thermonic safety valve installed, and you'll just get an "E" on the screen or a snotty message like INVALID INPUT FUNCTION. This is because when you pushed SHIFT and sin the calculator was expecting a fraction of less than 1. What it didn't expect was a whopping great big 42 and that's why it exploded.

$\sin^{-1}42 = E$ and the "E" stands for explosion

Of course if your calculator doesn't have a thermonic safety valve installed ... well, that's why you've got a fire extinguisher handy.

AHA! SO YOUR CALCULATOR'S BLOWING UP, IS IT? WELL THE FIENDISH ANGLETRON COMES WITH A SAFETY VALVE AND A FREE FIRE EXTINGUISHER!

To stop anything dangerous happening when you're playing with sines, try to remember this rule:

**Only give the SHIFT some action
when you're putting in a fraction.**

In other words, if you want to put a fraction into the calculator to get degrees, then push the SHIFT before the sin. But if you're putting in degrees, *don't* push SHIFT.

WHY CAN'T YOU HAVE A SIN THAT'S BIGGER THAN 1?

Simple. Remember that sin = $\frac{\text{opposite}}{\text{hypotenuse}}$ and that the hypotenuse is the longest side of a triangle. Therefore, the hypotenuse is always going to be bigger than the opposite side, so your fraction will always be less than 1.

### Some famous angles in trig

Nearly all values for sin, cos and tan are long complicated decimals, but a few of them are special.

**sin30° = 0·5 *exactly!***
We can see how this has to be true.

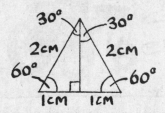

Here's an equilateral triangle, which means it has three angles of 60° and all its sides are the same length. To make things simple we've made each side measure 2 cm. The clever bit is that there's a line chopping it into two right-angled triangles. You can see that the 60° angle at the top has been split into two angles of 30°. You can also see that the side opposite the 30° angle is 1cm long and the hypotenuse is 2 cm long. As sin = $\frac{\text{opposite}}{\text{hypotenuse}}$, if we take the measurements off this little picture we get sin30° = $\frac{1\,\text{cm}}{2\,\text{cm}}$ = 0·5.

The sum sin30° = 0·5 always works. It doesn't matter how big or small your right-angled triangle is, as long as it has an angle of 30° you know that the side opposite the angle will always be exactly half as long as the hypotenuse. If you remember the bit we did about ratios, you can say the ratio of the opposite side to the hypotenuse is always 1:2. Look at this lot:

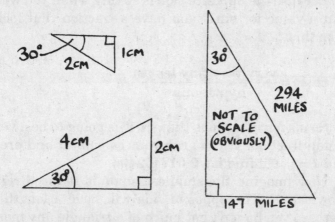

Even with the triangle that's measured in miles, if you work out 147 ÷ 294 you'll get the answer 0·5 because the angle is 30°.

If you've got a 30° set square (that's the skinny one) then get your ruler and measure the shortest side and the hypotenuse. It doesn't matter if your set square is a big one or a small one, you should find that the hypotenuse is twice as long. If you don't then you've got a wonky set square.

**sin0° and sin90°**

Imagine you've got a right-angled triangle and the smallest angle is 1°. You get a VERY long thin triangle and the opposite side will have a length of almost zero.

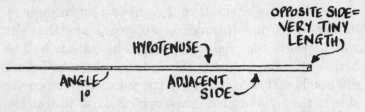

Because the opposite side is so tiny, when you work out a value for sin1° you have a fraction that looks like this:

$$\sin 1° = \frac{\text{very very tiny length}}{\text{hypotenuse}}$$

So it's fairly obvious that sin1° is going to be a very small fraction. If you grab your calculator and press *sin 1* = you'll find it's 0·017452406.

Now imagine the smallest angle is reduced right down to 0°. The opposite side will have a length of zero, so you haven't got much of a triangle any more. You'll just have two lines that run along on top of each other wondering where the third line went. Anyway, that's not important. What is important is this:

$$\sin 0° = \frac{\text{zero}}{\text{hypotenuse}} = 0$$

OK, now we'll open the angle right out up to 89°.

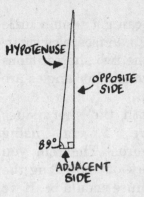

HYPOTENUSE

OPPOSITE SIDE

89°

ADJACENT SIDE

This time the opposite side is almost the same length as the hypotenuse, so your sin fraction is going to be very nearly equal to 1. If you check by pressing *sin 89 =* you'll find it's 0·999847695. When you open the angle up one more degree to 90°, the opposite side will be the same length as the hypotenuse. So guess what sin90° is?

$$\sin 90° = \frac{\text{same as hypotenuse}}{\text{hypotenuse}} = 1$$

YOU DON'T NEED TO UNDERSTAND ANY OF THIS!

Again, you can check this by pressing *sin 90 =* but be warned. If your calculator doesn't have a thermonic safety valve, don't press *tan 90 =* by accident or...

The FIENDISH ANGLETRON

THE MEASURING MACHINE OF YOUR DREAMS

## sin45°

There's one more sin value we can get from a little diagram and that's sin45°. Here's an isosceles right-angled triangle, which means the two shorter sides are the same length and the two smaller angles are both 45°.

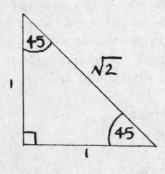

If both the short sides measure 1 cm, using Pythagoras' Theorem you can work out how long the hypotenuse should be. If we call the hypotenuse "h" the equation is: $1^2 + 1^2 = h^2$. As $1^2 = 1$ this equation becomes $1 + 1 = h^2$ and so $h^2 = 2$ and therefore $h = \sqrt{2}$. (We won't bother working out what $\sqrt{2}$ is just yet.)

If we choose one of the 45° angles we can see that sin45° = $\frac{\text{opposite}}{\text{hypotenuse}}$ = $\frac{1}{\sqrt{2}}$. Now you can see if your calculator is behaving itself, because if we work out $\frac{1}{\sqrt{2}}$ we should get exactly the same answer as sin45°. Try it.

● Press *sin 45* = and you should get 0·707106781.
● Press 1 ÷ $\sqrt{2}$ = and what do you get?

If the answers are not the same then your calculator has probably started rebelling, just like we warned you at the start of this book. The best thing to do is shove it screen-first into a smelly old sock and tell it that if it doesn't behave you'll feed it to the vacuum cleaner. Hah! That'll stop it getting grand ideas. Incidentally, an old sock and a vacuum cleaner is the perfect way to stop *anybody* getting grand ideas.

There, that should keep him busy for the rest of the chapter.

### Special cos angles

cos60° = 0·5

cos0° = 1

cos90° = 0

cos45° = sin45° = 0·707106781

If you really want to know why these results work, remember that if you've got two angles that add up to 90°, then the sin of one of them equals the cos of the other. This means that you can go through the last few pages, cross out "sin" and write "cos", cross out "opposite" and write "adjacent" and subtract any angle from 90°. That way you get all the full explanations and we save paper.

## Special tan angles

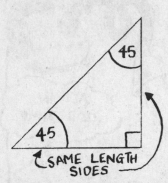

SAME LENGTH SIDES

There's only one worth mentioning and that's tan45° = 1. If you're going to have one 45° angle in a right-angled triangle, you have to have two of them because 45 + 45 + 90 =180. Therefore the triangle is isosceles which means the opposite and adjacent sides are equal, and so when you work out $T = \frac{O}{A}$ you get $tan45° = \frac{\text{same length}}{\text{same length}} = 1$.

PROD
PROD

GET AN ANGLETRON —BECAUSE YOU'RE WORTH IT...

## Getting sines without a calculator

If your calculator has been naughty and you're giving it the smelly-sock treatment, you can get sines without it. You won't be able to get loads of decimal places, but you can still get reasonable answers by doing some posh drawing instead. You need your ruler and protractor and also, to make life as easy as possible, you need some squared paper or graph paper. You make a diagram like this:

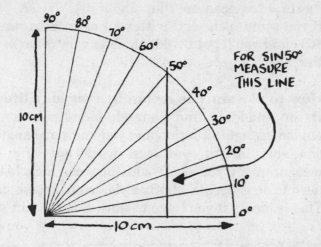

FOR SIN 50°
MEASURE
THIS LINE

You start by drawing a quarter circle that has a radius of 10 cm, then measure off any angles you might want with the protractor. (Our diagram is slightly smaller to fit in the book.)

Suppose you want to know what sin50° is? You draw a line from the 50° mark on the circle straight down to the bottom line. This line needs to be at right angles to the bottom line, which is why using squared paper helps. Now you measure this line accurately. It should be about 7·7 cm.

If you think about it, you've drawn a right-angled triangle like this:

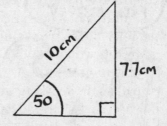

As sin $= \frac{O}{H}$ we can see that $\sin 50° = \frac{7 \cdot 7}{10} = 0 \cdot 77$.

If you want to check it with your calculator, push *sin 50 =* and you'll get $0 \cdot 766$ which is very close to what the diagram gave us.

## How to use sin, cos or tan in everyday life

If you suddenly find yourself faced with a right-angled triangle situation and you know one angle and one side length, you can work out any other measurement you want with just one sum. All you need to do is decide whether you need sin, cos or tan. This is handy if you have to work fast.

** NEWSFLASH**
The Evil Gollarks from the planet Zog have just popped into a garage and pumped up the air tanks on their home-made geometry set space avenger rocket...

97

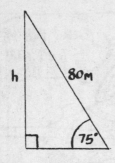

Look at the triangle diagram. We know the hypotenuse and the angle at the ground. The height is the line opposite the angle we know, so as we're working with the opposite and hypotenuse, we can find the height with just one sum using sin.

$\sin 75° = \frac{h}{80}$ and so: $h = 80 \times \sin 75° = 77\cdot27$

So the Gollarks are 77·27 metres above the ground.

THIS MIGHT NOT BE LONG ENOUGH, SIR.

HOW JOLLY AWKWARD. WE NEED A PLAN 'B'

POKE POKE

FREE AIR

TWIDDLE TWIDDLE

ARGH!

HOW TOPPING! HAVE SOME MEDALS!

SQURRRRRRRTHPPP

GOOD SHOW!

EEK!

FREE AIR

# The Fastbuck Gazette
## THE LEANING TOWER OF FASTBUCK

Citizens rejoice! Scum Products Ltd have just built their new factory chimney which stands a magnificent 40 metres high. Our worshipful mayor is celebrating by hosting a champagne party using the money that would otherwise have been wasted on building the chimney's foundations. At the party, the mayor said, "Is that chimney leaning over, or is it just me?"

Just for once the mayor is right. The chimney *is* leaning over, which isn't surprising! With no foundations to hold it steady, something dangerous was bound to happen, and it gets worse. In true Fastbuck style, the rubbish from the party has ended up blocking the waste pipe from the factory. While everyone is still outside celebrating, the whole building is gradually filling up with toxic scum. Soon it'll be dripping from the top of the chimney, but the question is, where will the scum hit the ground?

A quick measurement shows that the chimney is leaning at an angle of 62° so we can quickly draw a little diagram...

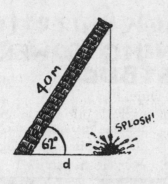

The scum will hit the ground directly underneath the end of the chimney, so we'll call the distance from here to the chimney base $d$. We can quickly work out what this is. The chimney is the hypotenuse of a right-angled triangle, and the distance $d$ is adjacent to the angle which we know is 62°. As the adjacent and hypotenuse are involved we use cos. We get:

$$\cos 62° = \frac{d}{40} \text{ and so } d = 40 \times \cos 62° = 18{\cdot}78 \text{ m}$$

So the scum is going to hit the ground 18·78 metres from the chimney base. Oh, look! The mayor is just about to make another speech. Where do you think we should put his podium?

## The Stones of Healing

As the sun was rising over the sands of the Forgotten Desert, a lone rider spurred her horse towards the craggy rock pile known as Golgarth Spike.

"Thag, Thag!" she shouted breathlessly. "Come on out, you puny little wart. Quick!"

High in the shadows of the rock pile was a small cave containing a small man with a big hat. Thag the mathemagician looked down towards the leather-clad woman who had leapt from her exhausted mount and was scrambling up the jagged steps towards him.

"Grizelda the Grisly!" said Thag. "Would you like a mushroom? They're awfully good."

Grizelda reached the top of the steps and glared at the small man. Grizelda's glare was famed throughout the Forgotten Desert. It was so fierce it made buffaloes weep and rattlesnakes bite their tongues and it had been known to cause trees to take a step backwards. But even though his head barely came past her shoulders, Thag was different. He was receiving a full-on, undiluted, maximum-impact, point-blank-range glare, and yet he simply smiled back and held out a mushroom.

"Thag, you're going to help me," Grizelda thundered. "Or else." She raised her double-stringed combat crossbow menacingly.

"Not today," said Thag. "I'm making mushroom jam. But thanks for calling by."

"Do you want your skin peeling off and feeding to the vultures?" snapped Grizelda.

"Sorry," said Thag turning away. "I've no time for your little pranks. Now do pop along like a good little barbarian."

101

"But, Thag," pleaded Grizelda. "We've found the Stones of Healing."

Thag turned back.

"Really?" asked Thag. "Where are they?"

"Here," said Grizelda, thrusting a piece of grubby parchment at him.

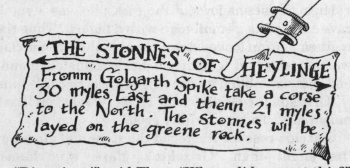

THE STONNES OF HEYLINGE
Fromm Golgarth Spike take a corse
30 myles East and thenn 21 myles
to the North. The Stonnes wil be
layed on the greene rock.

"Directions!" said Thag. "Where did you get this?"

Grizelda quickly explained. The previous day, her army had been having a friendly skirmish with Urgum the Axeman and his seventeen sons near Gibbet Tree. Afterwards, they had all been sitting around a fire and comparing their new scars when an old gypsy approached them. "Feed an old lady," she had begged, which sounded like a fun idea. In fact, they were just about to feed her to Urgum's pet bear when she screamed, "Stop! Let me go and I will give you something in return." The gypsy handed over two identical parchments. Urgum took one and Grizelda the other. "The healing stones!" Urgum had said. "Let's go together in the morning and find them."

"But when I woke up this morning, Urgum had already set off," wailed Grizelda.

"So that's what he was doing," said Thag. "He got here just before dawn and as soon as the sun broke over the eastern horizon, he set off towards it."

Grizelda peered across the desert plain and spotted a tiny dust cloud in the distance. "There he is!" she snarled. "He's riding east, and he must be two miles away. He double-crossed me!"

"Chase after him!" said Thag. "You're the fastest rider in the desert."

"Of course I am," said Grizelda. "But he's miles in front already, and if he saw me coming he'd race ahead."

"But suppose he didn't see you?"

"I've got it!" said Grizelda. "You must use your magic to make me invisible. Well, go on then, or I'll pluck your eyes out."

"Now now, Grizelda," chuckled Thag who was already tracing out a diagram on the sandy floor. "Ask nicely."

"If you help me, your head will not be on the end of a spear before sundown," promised Grizelda.

"If that's your best, it'll have to do," said Thag. "Now then, look at this."

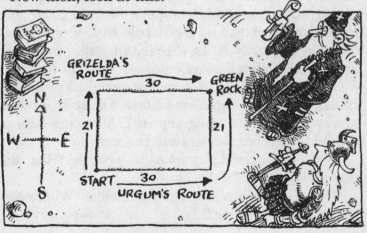

"Urgum will go 30 miles east and then 21 miles north," explained Thag. "In all, he must travel 51 miles."

"It'll take him all day," said Grizelda. "So, how do I become invisible?"

"You don't need to," said Thag. "First ride 21 miles north and then 30 miles east. It will take you to the stones a different way. Urgum will never see you. If you go fast you'll get there before him."

"Ha!" said Grizelda. "That'll teach him."

Grizelda charged down the steps, leapt on to her horse and was away.

"Just a simple *please* or *thank you* would have been nice," muttered Thag to himself. "And I'd rather like to have the Stones of Healing for myself..."

Thag reached for a large book full of numbers and studied it very carefully. After he had made a few notes, he opened up a weathered leather bag and pulled out a magnetic compass. He set it on the ground and watched as the needle swung round the dial to point north. As he checked the other numbers around the dial, a big smile appeared on his face.

Later in the day, after several long, hard hours' riding, Grizelda's exhausted horse finally staggered to a stop beside a large green rock. Moments later a second horse approached from the south.

"Grizelda!" cursed Urgum as he saw her. "How did you get here first?"

"Never mind that!" snapped Grizelda. "Where are the Stones of Healing?"

They looked around in vain.

"All I can find is this!" said Urgum. He pointed at a hollow in the green rock. Resting on it was a single mushroom.

"Thag!" gasped Grizelda. "But I left him back at his cave!"

As night fell, Thag was tying his pony up to the tree below his steps. It had been a long ride, but an immensely rewarding one, even if it had given him quite a headache. He climbed up to the cave entrance and poured himself a goblet of water. Reaching into his bag, he took out a small white circular healing stone. With a swig and a gulp, he swallowed it. In a few minutes he felt much better.

"Thank goodness for healing stones," he sighed. "Or aspirins, as I like to call them."

So how did Thag beat both Urgum and Grizelda without them seeing him?

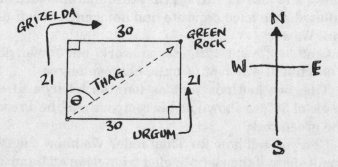

The answer is that Thag rode in a straight line to the green rock. Here we can see the routes that Grizelda and Urgum took to reach the green rock, but Thag realized he could take a direct route, which was much shorter.

All he needed to know was the exact direction he needed to ride, which is marked with a "θ". (θ is a Greek letter called *theta* and it's used a lot when people don't know what angles are.) His compass would show him where north was, and the dial on the compass is marked in degrees, and would indicate any other direction he wanted. If you don't know about compasses, there's a full explanation of them coming up on page 181.

We can show Grizelda's route by making a right-angled triangle like this:

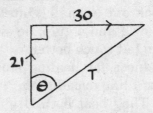

We can see that the side opposite the angle is 30 miles, and also we can see that the adjacent side is 21 miles. As we have opposite and adjacent, we can use tan. We get:

$\tan\theta = \frac{30}{21} = 1{\cdot}429$. So to work out $\theta$ we get: $\theta = \tan^{-1}1{\cdot}429 = 55°$ (to the nearest degree).

Thag worked out that as long as he rode at an angle of 55°, as shown on his compass dial, he'd reach the green rock.

Can you tell how far Thag rode? We know the two small sides of the right-angled triangle are 21 and 30, so if we call the distance $T$, then Pythagoras' Theorem says that $T^2 = 30^2 + 21^2 = 900 + 441 = 1341$. So Thag rode for $\sqrt{1341}$, which is 36·6 miles – over 14 miles less than Urgum or Grizelda, all thanks to the power of trig.

Oh yawn ... but he's right as usual. Can you see why Thag didn't ride 36·6 miles? You don't need Pythagoras or a calculator to work this out!

### The weird old words of trig

Now that everybody has got used to calculators, we take long tricky sums for granted. It's also very easy to get values for sin, cos and tan. We just push a few buttons and – *ting!* – there's the answer to as many decimal places as you can be bothered with. What's more, you don't really care how many calculations you need to do because it's all over in a matter of seconds.

However, in the olden days everything had to be worked out by hand, and if you had to divide by long decimals it could take *hours*. Even looking up trig values meant staring at pages of tiny numbers and working out what you needed. After all that you'd probably end up with the decimal point in the wrong place anyway.

It's not surprising then that people were desperate to cut down on the amount of work they had to do. Look at this classic little problem...

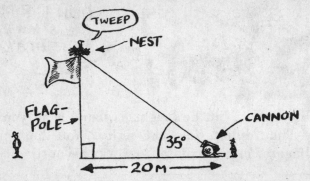

Colonel Cancel is preparing for a royal visit but to his horror he discovers that there's a buzzard's nest at the top of his flagpole. He decides to remove it by aiming his cannon at the nest. He knows that the cannon is 20 metres from the base of the flagpole and that the angle of elevation is 35°.

What he needs to know is how much gunpowder to put in the cannon, and for that he needs to know exactly how far the cannonball must fly.

**fig 2 :** Too much powder.

EEK!

SPADGE

YIKES! MUMMY!

If $f$ is how far the cannonball flies, this is the hypotenuse of a right-angled triangle. We know that the side adjacent to the 35° angle is 20 m so using $C = \frac{A}{H}$ we can put $\cos 35° = \frac{20}{f}$. If we multiply both sides by $f$ we get $f \times \cos 35° = 20$ and then if we divide both sides by $\cos 35°$ we finally get:

$$f = \frac{20}{\cos 35}$$

This is dead easy with a modern calculator. You just push in $20 \div \cos 35°$ = and the answer leaps straight out and kisses you on the nose. However, in the olden days you'd have to start by looking up $\cos 35°$ and the closest answer you'd probably get would have been 0·8192. You would then need to work out $20 \div 0·8192$ ... eeek!

With a bit of careful planning, people found an easier way to do sums like this. They made extra tables which showed values of $\frac{1}{\sin}$, $\frac{1}{\cos}$ and $\frac{1}{\tan}$ which are called **secant, cosecant and cotangent** or sec, csc and cot for short.

So in the olden days you'd solve the colonel's problem by starting with $f = \frac{20}{\cos35}$ which is the same as $f = 20 \times \frac{1}{\cos35}$. The clever bit is that $\frac{1}{\cos35}$ = csc35. Therefore, the sum becomes $f = 20 \times$ csc35.

Instead of looking up cos35° in the tables, you would have turned to the cosecant page and looked up csc35° which would have come out as 1·221. Once you'd got that, all you needed to do was the much simpler sum of 20 × 1·221 which comes out as 24·42.

Three more words you'd find in the tables were **arcsin, arccos** and **arctan**. "Arc" in front of sin, cos or tan means the same as "inverse", so **arcsin** is the same as $\sin^{-1}$. In other words, if you know that:

sin30° = 0·5

you can put it the other way round by saying:

arcsin0·5 = 30°

You can also have **arccos** = $\cos^{-1}$ or even **arctan** = $\tan^{-1}$ and guess what? They also had **arcsec, arccsc** and **arccot**, and of course there were separate tables of numbers for all of these too.

We're so lucky that we've got calculators these days, but it's a bit sad that you don't see grand old words like "arccos" much any more. Many generations of maths heroes spent years preparing all the different tables, and these tables were used to invent some of the greatest achievements of humanity – including the calculators that put them out of business. How unfair can you get?

# SUPERSIN AND COSGIRL

TUM TE TUM...

M

3

6·5

By now you'll realize that right-angled triangles are completely at our mercy. Thanks to the power of trig we can grab something like this and work out the mystery angle $M$ in a flash. We know the lengths of the opposite and hypotenuse sides, so we use sin. We get: $\sin M = \frac{3}{6\cdot5}$ and so we work out $\sin^{-1}\frac{3}{6\cdot5}$ by pushing $3 \div 6\cdot5 = INV\ sin =$ on the calculator and we find that $M = 27\cdot49°$.

Hang on – who's that in the distance? Oh no, Professor Fiendish is following us and he smells rather old sock-ish. Doubtless he's still trying to get rid of his silly Angletron.

I'VE FITTED A FEW EXTRA FEATURES!

See how desperate he's getting? Why on Earth would we need to buy his ridiculous machine when we've got a bit of trig and a calculator?

Eek! What's he done? He's stamped the "3" side down a bit and flattened the right angle out to 110°. What's worse, the other angles in the triangle have changed too! How diabolical.

Keep calm. Although we've lost our nice right angle, don't be fooled into thinking that the only way to work out the angles accurately is to pay him for his confounded machine. Oh no, he hasn't beaten us yet. It's time to summon the awesome power of SUPERSIN.

## The Supersin formula

Here comes Supersin with his awesome formula, so we're saved. Thanks to him we can escape the confines of right-angled triangles. The supersin formula doesn't look like any other formula you've ever seen before. You'll notice it's got *three* bits connected by two equals signs! There are two versions:

For some reason Supersin himself seems to be dripping wet, but we'll try to ignore that. Instead, let's see where all the a, b and c bits come from.

On this triangle the angles are marked A, B and C and the lengths of the sides are marked a, b, and c. You'll notice that side a is opposite angle A, side b is opposite angle B and side c is opposite angle C. This makes for a simple way of putting triangle lines and angles into formulas.

The sin formula says that you can get *any* triangle, and pick one of

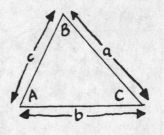

the angles. Work out the sin of the angle and divide by the opposite side. It doesn't matter which of the three angles you pick, when you work out the sin then divide by the opposite side, you'll always get the same answer!

This means that we can find our mystery angle $M$ now, even after the Professor squashed the right angle into 110°.

Thanks to Supersin we don't need any silly machines. Here's what we've got:

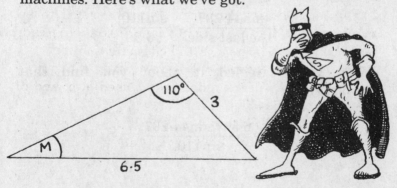

Although we don't know all the angles and sides, we can see that the angle opposite the 6·5 side is 110°. What's more, the angle opposite the 3 side is the one we want – $M$. We can make a little version of the sin formula with just two bits:

115

$$\frac{\sin M}{3} = \frac{\sin 110}{6 \cdot 5}$$

Multiply both sides of the equation by 3 to get:

$$\sin M = \frac{3 \times \sin 110}{6 \cdot 5}$$

To work this out on a calculator you first work out the right-hand side by pushing *3 × sin 110 ÷ 6·5 =* and that tells you that $\sin M = 0 \cdot 433704286$. All you do now is push *SHIFT sin =* and you get the answer that angle $M = 25 \cdot 703°$.

If we wanted to go mad we could also work out what the other angle is because $180° - 110° - 25 \cdot 703° = 44 \cdot 297°$. Then we could work out the length of the last side if we really wanted to because

$$\frac{\sin 44 \cdot 297}{\text{the last side}} = \frac{\sin 110}{6 \cdot 5}.$$

When you've jiggled it about you find that the last side =

$$\frac{6 \cdot 5 \times \sin 44 \cdot 297}{\sin 110}.$$

But right now we can't be bothered to finish it off as we're far too busy laughing at the Professor who's sulking because we don't need his Angletron. We can get all the sides and angles in *any* triangle we want.

Oh, no! Surely our superhero can't be beaten? The Professor has produced a triangle that only has one marked angle, and we don't know the opposite side! If we put the bits we know into the sin formula we get:

$$\frac{\sin 54}{a} = \frac{\sin B}{5} = \frac{\sin C}{4 \cdot 5}$$

We can only solve anything with the sin formula if one of the fractions has numbers we know on the top *and* the bottom. Curses! If only we knew the length of line $a$ we could sort everything else out, but we don't.

117

118

## The cosine formula

$$a^2 = b^2 + c^2 - 2bc\cos A$$

This formula might not be pretty, but it's just what we need right now! (Although Cosgirl looks like she needs a towel too. Best not to ask why.) If you know two lines of a triangle and the angle between them, thanks to this formula you can find the length of the third line. Angle $A$ is the angle we know and lines $b$ and $c$ are the lines we know. $a$ is the line we want to find out about.

If you check the Professor's last triangle, the angle we know is 54° so we'll make that $A$ in the formula. The two sides we know measure 5 and 4·5, so we make these into $b$ and $c$. (It doesn't matter which one is $b$ and which is $c$.) If we put these values in the formula we can get $a$.

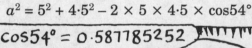

$$a^2 = 5^2 + 4\cdot5^2 - 2 \times 5 \times 4\cdot5 \times \cos54°$$

$$a^2 = 25 + 20{\cdot}25 - 45 \times 0{\cdot}5878$$

$$a^2 = 45{\cdot}25 - 26{\cdot}451 = 18{\cdot}799$$

And therefore $a = \sqrt{18{\cdot}799} = 4{\cdot}336.$

NOW LET'S SEE THE TRIANGLE, PROFESSOR!

If we want the other angles we just use the sin formula again:

$$\frac{\sin 54}{4{\cdot}336} = \frac{\sin B}{5} = \frac{\sin C}{4{\cdot}5}$$

At last! Let's just take the first two bits:

$$\frac{\sin 54}{4{\cdot}336} = \frac{\sin B}{5}$$

A quick shuffle gives us:

$$\sin B = \frac{5 \times \sin 54}{4 \cdot 336} = 0 \cdot 932907$$

and therefore angle $B = \sin^{-1} 0 \cdot 932907 = 68 \cdot 89°$.

For angle $C$ it's simple as we know $C = 180 - A - B$, therefore $C = 180 - 54 - 68 \cdot 89 = 57 \cdot 11°$.

What's this? There are no angles marked – all we know are the three sides. The sin formula is no use until we know one of the angles, so can we use the cos formula?

Wow! She's shuffled the cos formula around so that if we know the three sides of the triangle, we can work out any of the angles. If we want angle $A$ we can use the numbers off this diagram and put them in the new formula...

$$\cos A = \frac{7^2 + 4^2 - 5^2}{2 \times 4 \times 7}$$

and when you bash this through you get $A = 44 \cdot 42°$.

Once we've got one angle, we can use the sin formula to work out the others, or you can fiddle around with the letters in the new cos formula to get:

$$\cos B = \frac{a^2 + c^2 - b^2}{2ac} \text{ and } \cos C = \frac{a^2 + b^2 - c^2}{2ab}$$

BAH! ANGLE A WAS EASY, BUT I BET YOU GET ANGLE B WRONG!

Why should angle B be a problem? Let's try it and have a look at what happens:

$$\cos B = \frac{5^2 + 4^2 - 7^2}{2 \times 5 \times 4} = \frac{-8}{40} = -0 \cdot 2$$

Ooh, look – we've got a minus sign! Don't panic, this is one of the really clever bits about the cos formula. The minus sign tells your calculator that the angle is obtuse (i.e. more than 90°). So when you work out $B = \cos^{-1} -0 \cdot 2$ you get $B = 101 \cdot 54°$ which is correct.

123

124

## The tan polygon formula

Here's something VERY different from what we've seen so far. Instead of triangles we're going to have a quick look at regular polygons. If you've read *Vicious Circles and Other Savage Shapes* you'll know that a regular polygon is a shape with all its sides the same length and angles the same size. Here are a few:

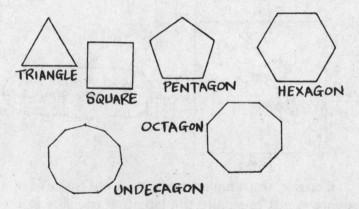

After *Vicious Circles* came out, several Murderous Maths readers asked us what an eleven-sided shape is called – well now you know. We were also asked if there was a formula to work out the *area* of any regular polygon. There *is* such a formula which even works with undecagons (although why anyone would want to know the area of an undecagon completely beats us), but be warned, it's not exactly cuddly. However you asked for it so you've only got yourselves to blame...

$$\text{area of regular polygon} = \frac{ns^2}{4\tan(\frac{180}{n})}$$

$n$ = the number of sides your polygon has
$s$ = how long each side is

We can test this with the simplest polygon – a square. Let's say each side measures 7 cm.

Of course, the simple way to work out the area of a square is just to square the length of one side so the area is $7^2 = 49$ sq cm. Now let's see if the formula gives the same result. We swap $n$ for 4 and $s$ for 7 and we get:

$$\text{Area of square} = \frac{4 \times 7^2}{4\tan(\frac{180}{4})} = \frac{4 \times 49}{4\tan(45)}$$

By now you might remember that tan45° = 1 so this becomes:

Area of square = $\frac{4 \times 49}{4 \times 1}$ = 49 sq cm.

The formula answer agrees with the simple answer, so it works!

Squares are easy, but if you had a septagon with its seven sides measuring 3 cm each, what would the area be? Let's see what it looks like first:

*Oi, Poskitt, is there a quick way to draw a septagon?*

Pah. You'd think our murderous artist Mr Reeve had done enough of these books by now to work out a few shortcuts for himself. You just get a 20p coin out of your pocket, plonk it on the paper and put a tiny pencil dot at each corner. Take away the coin and join them up.

*Lend me 20p then. I only have £20 notes.*

There, that's what a septagon looks like, and you'll just have to pretend that the sides each measure 3 cm. So to get the area you use the formula and make $n = 7$ and $s = 3$. Off we go:

$$\text{Area of septagon} = \frac{7 \times 3^2}{4\tan(\frac{180}{7})} = \frac{7 \times 9}{4 \times 0.482} = \frac{63}{1.926}$$

$$= 32.71 \text{ sq cm}$$

GOOD BOY, TANDOG!

IF WE'RE DOING AREAS, I'VE GOT ONE MORE FORMULA FOR YOU!

### The sin triangle area formula

William Shakepeare wasn't too well known for his mathematical prowess, so when he had to include this formula in his long forgotten play *Henry XII part 5*, it went like this:

*Act VIII scene 27*

Trigonomo (a servant):

*If a triangle has no right angle*
*And the area needs to be seen,*
*Multiply half by two of the sides*
*And the sin of the angle between.*

Lady Radiana:

*Fie, fool, and get thee gone with thy clumsy rhymes ere I perforate thine buttcheeks with my dividers.*

*(exeunt)*

Here's what Trigonomo was trying to say:

## Area of triangle = $\frac{1}{2}bc \sin A$

The formula looks tough but actually it's really handy. The usual formula for triangle areas is $\frac{1}{2}$ × base × height. This is fine if you have a right-angled triangle because you just pick one of the shorter sides to be the base and then the other short side is the height.

area = $\frac{1}{2}$ × 4 × 5 = 10

All nice and easy with the right angle there, but suppose instead of 90° it was just 70°? For the usual formula you need to know the perpendicular height which we've marked on the next page as *h*.

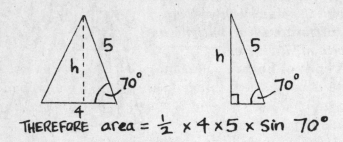

area $= \frac{1}{2} \times 4 \times h$    $\sin 70° = \frac{h}{5}$ and so $h = 5 \times \sin 70°$

THEREFORE area $= \frac{1}{2} \times 4 \times 5 \times \sin 70°$

These pictures show you how the sin formula comes about. You can work out the height $h$ using sin because there's a little right-angled triangle with 5 as the hypotenuse and $h$ as the opposite side. So you have $\sin 70° = \frac{h}{5}$. This turns into $h = 5 \times \sin 70°$.

Now you know how to get $h$ you just need to put this into the area formula which is area $= \frac{1}{2} \times$ base $\times$ height. As the base is 4 and $h = 5 \times \sin 70°$ we know the area is $\frac{1}{2} \times 4 \times 5 \times \sin 70°$. If you work this one out you get:

$$\frac{1}{2} \times 4 \times 5 \times \sin 70° = 9 \cdot 40 \text{ sq cm}$$

This is the same as what Trigonomo said: "multiply half by two of the sides and the sin of the angle between". Here the two sides are 4 and 5 and the angle between them is 70°.

There are loads more formulas using the super powers of sin, cos and tan, but we've already asked enough of our trigometric superheroes, so it's time to bid them farewell.

## A spot of bother

Be honest, a few things in this book have probably been bothering you for a while, so we'll try to clear them up now.

- The borrowed 20p coin. No further sightings so far. We presume it's lost somewhere along the long dank corridors in the deepest vaults of Mr Reeve's wallet.
- The CAT triangle on page 41. Joking aside – how did we make sure those angles and lengths were so accurate? No, it wasn't really by drawing and measuring. When we were putting the book together we used the sin and cosine formulas!
- And finally, as we wave farewell to our trigonometric superheroes, just one question remains. Why did they arrive soaking wet? Could it be some clue as to their secret identities? Maybe we'll never know.

# THE 13TH HOLE TRIANGULATION CHALLENGE

Now we've met the sin formula, we'll have a look at a trick called **triangulation** which is so neat and groovy that it's got a little chapter all to itself. It sounds murderous but actually it's a simple method of judging how far away objects are. If you've got two eyes on the front of your head, then you've been doing it all your life!

Hold your finger out in front of you at arm's length and look at it. Now bring your finger towards you. You can see it's getting closer because your finger is looking bigger but, more importantly, your eyeballs are having to swivel round to see it.

If you draw a triangle between your two eyes and your finger, you'll see that the angles at your eyes get smaller as the finger gets closer. Your brain automatically calculates a triangle using these angles and the distance between your eyes, and that's how it judges how far away your finger is. Therefore, as you'll appreciate, one of the main uses of triangulation is that it stops you poking yourself in the eye.

We can use a much bigger version of triangulation to take on an almost impossible mission. You'll need to put on your silliest trousers and sickliest jumper, leap on to the buggy and head off to the land of double bogies, because – *hurrah* – we're taking a jaunt across the Murderous Maths executive golf course.

The problem concerns the 13th hole. There is a special prize for anybody who can find out exactly how far it is from the tee shot to the flag, and many people have suffered a glorious range of ghastly fates trying to measure it. Here's why:

Here's the equipment we'll need:

- Something to mark out a long length. We've got a rope that's 40 m long.
- A long straight stick
- A protractor
- A calculator

All we need to do is set out a great big triangle. We start by putting one end of the rope at the tee-shot position, then laying the rest of the rope down in a straight line along the cliff top. We know the rope is 40 m long, and this will be known as the baseline of our triangle.

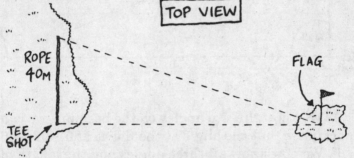

Next we go back to the tee-shot end of the rope and measure the angle between the rope and the flag. Lie the long stick on the ground at the end of the rope so that it points directly to the flag.

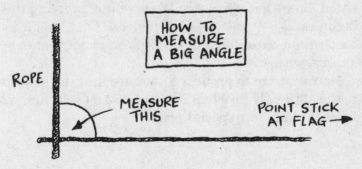

Then we measure the angle between the stick and the rope with the protractor and find that it's 92°. Next we go and measure the angle between the other end of the rope and the flag using the stick in the same way. We find that it's 86° so all we need to do now is draw a diagram of the triangle.

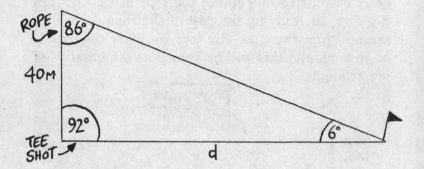

As we know the two angles on the baseline, we can quickly see that the angle at the flag is $180 - 92 - 86 = 6°$. We now know all three angles and the length of the base line, so we can work out $d$ (the distance of the flag from the tee shot) using the sin formula. Remember, you put the sin of the angle over the length of the opposite side, and they should all be equal. So we get $\frac{\sin 6}{40} = \frac{\sin 86}{d}$. With a bit of juggling this becomes: $d = \frac{40 \times \sin 86}{\sin 6} = 381.7$ metres! That was a lot easier than scrambling down cliffs and being eaten by sharks, wasn't it?

Now it's time to proudly announce that the answer to the 13th-hole problem is about 382 metres, and we want to claim our special prize.

# TINY ANGLES AND MEGA TRIANGLES

You might think that an angle of 1° is really tiny, but there are lots of times when people need to use angles that are much smaller. Things get rather strange with really tiny angles, including the odd fact that sin and tan become almost the same thing. What's even odder is that we start to use…

## Minutes and seconds

When people send rockets across space they need to measure angles really accurately, so sometimes they split degrees into minutes and seconds! There are 60 "minutes" in one degree and 60 "seconds" in one minute. Just so that you don't confuse this with minutes and seconds on a clock, they get called **arcminutes** and **arcseconds**. You indicate arcminutes with one little apostrophe like this: '. Arcseconds are shown with a double apostrophe like this: ". Here's how it all works out:

$$1° = 60' = 3600''$$

Suppose you have an angle of 17·724°. You can convert the 0·724 of a degree into arcminutes and arcseconds. As there are 60 arcminutes in one degree, the number of arcminutes in 0·724 of a degree is 0·724 × 60 = 43·44'. You then need to convert the 0·44 of an arcminute into arcseconds. As there are 60 arcseconds in one arcminute, the number of arcseconds in 0·44 of an arcminute is 0·44 × 60 = 26·4". Therefore 17·724° is the same as 17° and 43' and 26·4″ and we can write it like this: 17° 43′ 26·4″.

Using arcminutes and arcseconds is called the **sexagesimal** system, and usually it only turns up when you're describing the exact positions of stars and planets in the sky. (Thank goodness!)

### How to draw one arcsecond

As you know, one degree is pretty small and one arcminute is $\frac{1}{60}$ of a degree, which is so small it's starting to get silly. One arcsecond is $\frac{1}{60}$ of an arcminute, which is seriously ridiculous. If you want to draw one single arcsecond, draw a triangle with two lines that are each 1 *kilometre* long and make the third line that joins them up 4·848 *millimetres* long. The angle between the two long lines will be 0° 0′ 1″.

Another way to draw an angle of 0° 0′ 1″ is to use the sun, a stick and a stopwatch. Stick a long thin stick into a flat piece of ground then, as the sun moves across the sky, the shadow of the stick will slowly move around. Now get ready, because you're going to have to act FAST.

Start your stopwatch and then very quickly draw a line running from the base of the stick along to the end of the shadow. Then 0·066667 of a second later, draw a second line along the shadow. (0·066667 is $\frac{1}{15}$th of a second.) In that time, the shadow will have moved 0° 0′ 1″, therefore the angle between your two lines will be 0° 0′ 1″.

Do you want to know how we worked this out? We could answer that question for you but it isn't very interesting. Really, truly and honestly you don't want to know. Or do you? We're warning you, interesting it is NOT, but just in case you're a heavy sums addict we'd hate to deprive you...

The Earth does one complete rotation every 24 hours, which gives the effect of the sun moving around us once in 24 hours. If you're at the North pole in June or at the South pole in December, the sun never sets. It just goes round in a circle in the sky. (Sorry, that was slightly interesting. We'll get back to the heavy sums now.) Therefore, the sun seems to move a full circle, which is 360° in 24 hours.

Here come the sums:

- How many arcseconds are there in a circle?
  There are 360° in a circle, each degree has 60 arcminutes and each arcminute has 60 arcseconds. We get 360 × 60 × 60 = 1,296,000″.

- How many seconds (of time) are there in a day?
  There are 24 hours in a day, each hour has 60 minutes and each minute has 60 seconds, so there are 24 × 60 × 60 = 86,400 seconds.

- So how many seconds does the sun take to move round one arcsecond?
  It travels 1,296,000″ in 86,400 seconds. Therefore to travel 1″ it takes $\frac{86,400}{1,296,000}$ = 0·0666667 or $\frac{1}{15}$ seconds.

**The ° ′ ″ or *dms* calculator button**

Multiplying and dividing by 60 and 3600 is really tedious, but if you ever need to do it, some calculators have a degrees-minutes-seconds button which does the conversions for you. It's probably marked like this: ° ′ ″ – or it has the letters *dms*. (If your calculator doesn't have one of these buttons, maybe you can borrow the ° ′ ″ button off somebody else's calculator and stick it on yours for this section.)

If you want to convert an angle of 31·2367° you just put it into your calculator, and then you'll probably need to push the "=" button. Now push your ° ′ ″ button. Wahey! You should get something like: 31° 14′ 12·1″.

If you want to convert something like 49° 35′ 41″ back into a decimal, then you have to put each number into the calculator and push the ° ′ ″ button after it. When you've pushed the ° ′ ″ button for the third time, push = to tell the calculator you've finished or it'll get worried. Then you push the ° ′ ″ button once more and you should get the answer in degrees. In this case it should be 49·5947°. If you push the ° ′ ″ button at the wrong time, then bang goes another calculator. (Unless it's got the thermonic safety valve in which case you'll get a message saying "Don't be silly" or something.)

Incidentally, if you're doing a sum involving time and you get an answer like 12·4923 hours, then you can use the ° ′ ″ button to convert it into hours, minutes and seconds in the same way. You just put in 12·4923 then push = then push the ° ′ ″ button and you get 12 hrs 29 mins 32 secs.

# How good are your eyes?

We'll just pop over to the desert to try a night-time experiment. You'll notice a car is coming towards us from a long distance away. The headlights are on but when the car is a really long way away, they merge together to look like one point of light. Obviously when the car has reached us, you will be able to see both headlights clearly. But how far away will the car be when you can first make out both headlights separately? If your eyes are about average, it should be about 2·5 km (or 1·5 miles), but how did we work that out?

The answer is that the human eye can "resolve" angles to about 2 arcminutes. (People with brilliant eyesight can resolve right down to 1 arcminute or even less.) This all sounds a bit complicated until you see a diagram:

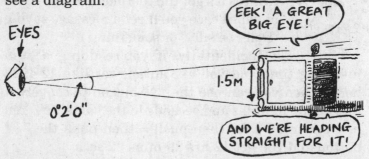

EEK! A GREAT BIG EYE!

EYES

1·5M

0°2'0"

AND WE'RE HEADING STRAIGHT FOR IT!

Here you can see two lines coming out of an eye – the angle between them is 2 arcminutes. (Obviously we've made the angle bigger in the diagram, otherwise the two lines would just look like they were on top of each other.) The lines reach the headlights of a car, which we've measured as being 1·5 m apart. If the angle made between the two headlights and the eye were any smaller than 2 arcminutes, most normal people wouldn't be able to distinguish two separate lights.

All we need to do now is to work out how long the other two lines of this triangle are, and we'll start with a little bit of CHEATING. When you get a triangle with an angle of less than $\frac{1}{2}°$, then you can pretend one of the other angles is a right angle if you like. It hardly affects the answer at all and it makes the sums much easier! Let's quickly convert this into a right-angled triangle:

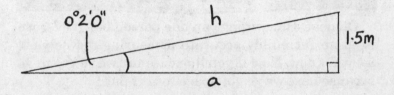

We can now work out the distance between the eye and the headlights and the odd thing is that you can choose either sin or tan. This is because with really tiny angles (e.g. less than $\frac{1}{2}°$), they give almost the same results. Remember that sin = $\frac{\text{opposite}}{\text{hypotenuse}}$ and tan = $\frac{\text{opposite}}{\text{adjacent}}$ . Here the hypotenuse (marked $h$) and the adjacent (marked $a$) sides are almost identical, so let's try them both.

- $\sin 2' = \frac{1 \cdot 5}{h}$ therefore $h = \frac{1 \cdot 5}{\sin 2'} = 2578$ m.
- $\tan 2' '' = \frac{1 \cdot 5}{a}$ therefore $a = \frac{1 \cdot 5}{\tan 2'} = 2578$ m.

(If you haven't got a ° ′ ″ button, then $2' = \frac{1}{30}° = 0 \cdot 03333°$, so you can try using $\sin 0 \cdot 03333°$ and $\tan 0 \cdot 03333°$ instead.)

Whether we use sin or tan we get an answer of about 2,500 m which is 2·5 km. That's how far away the car was when we could first make out both headlamps, but it's a lot closer now...

Oh dear. How wrong can one person be? If ever we need an incredibly accurate measuring device we'll let you know. Now if you'll excuse us, we've got to go because next we've got space to sort out.

### Tiny angles in a big universe

Down on Earth, an angle of 1° usually seems too pathetic to bother anyone, but, if you start looking at the night sky, 1° becomes a great big massive clunky scary thing. That's when arcminutes and arcseconds start to be really useful. You'll get an idea of how small some of the angles in space are by looking at the full moon.

144

You can't tell how big the moon is or how far away it is just by looking at it. All you can tell is the *apparent diameter* which is the angle of your vision that the moon occupies.

This picture shows the angle we're talking about, so how big do you think the angle is? Go on, have a guess...

- 30°
- 10°
- 3°
- 1°
- $\frac{1}{2}$° (or 0° 30') ?

You might find it hard to believe, but the moon only takes up about half a degree!

So how many moons would it take to make a complete bracelet of moons going right round the Earth? As the bracelet goes right round 360° and each moon only takes up about $\frac{1}{2}$°, you'd need about 720 of them.

One of the strange things about living on Earth is that the sun and moon appear to be about the same size. This is because, although the sun is 400 times bigger than the moon, by sheer chance it is also 400 times further away. You can show this with two similar triangles, one being 400 times bigger than the other.

145

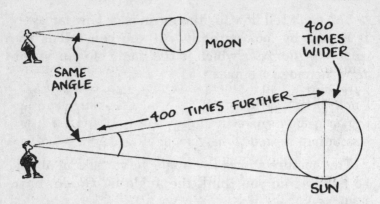

(We've only made the sun triangle about twice as big as the moon triangle here, otherwise this page would need to be about 18 metres wide.) As these triangles are similar, the angle of the apparent diameter is the same, and that's why the sun and the moon look the same size in the sky.

As it turns out, the moon is only about 380,000 km away, so we've managed to send a few rockets up there to check the distance and wrap a tape measure around it to see exactly how fat it is and so on. The sun is about 150,000,000 km away, which sounds a lot, but compared to the rest of space it's practically next door.

### The thumb and moon illusion

- Imagine it's a night when there is a full moon in the sky. You stick your arm straight out in front of you and put your thumb up. If you look through just one eye, do you think your thumbnail will be big enough to completely block the moon out? Have a think about it, then try it out. Better still, ask a friend what they think!

146

## How to find the distance of a star

The very tiniest angles and cleverest maths all come in handy when astronomers start studying stars that are billions and billions of kilometres away. Be warned, some of the sums and measurements that astronomers use are pretty gruesome even for a Murderous Maths book, so before we dive in we'll get in the mood with a jolly little experiment. It involves looking a bit silly, but who cares? If you're reading this book in a library or on the bus, don't be a wimp – JUST DO IT. Better still, pass this book to somebody else and make them do it. Ho ho, we do have our fun, don't we? Here we go then…

- Take one of your shoes and socks off then stick your leg out as far as you can in front of you with your big toe sticking up towards the opposite wall.

- Shut your left eye and hold out one arm with your thumb sticking up directly in front of your toe. Notice which bit of wall is behind your toe and thumb. Keep your leg and arm very steady.
- Now shut your right eye. Notice how dark it's got.
- Now open your left eye. You'll see that your toe seems to have moved across the wall. What's more, your thumb isn't in front of your toe any more, it's moved even further across! This is because you've looked at your toe and thumb from two slightly different positions, and this makes them seem to move across the background. As your thumb is nearer, it seems to have moved more.

Now we'll try the same experiment, but we're going to do it on a slightly bigger scale.

First of all you have to remember that in the olden days before telly, people used to spend a lot of the night time staring at the sky. (Oh, sorry – you can put your shoe and sock back on now.) Apart from the sun and moon, they quickly spotted a few other little bright objects that seemed to move around reasonably quickly – over the course of a year their positions would change quite a lot. They called these objects the "planets" (which means "wanderers") and, as you probably know, all the planets including Earth just whizz round the sun trying not to bash into each other. But what about all the other stars?

When the astronomers made really accurate maps of the star patterns they saw that these patterns were not exactly the same throughout the year. Mind you the differences were very tiny so it must have been rather dull just watching the sky waiting for telly to be invented. Of course, these days we're lucky because we do have telly so we can enjoy repeated comedies, miserable soaps, reality game shows, depressing news, desperate talent competitions, celebrity panel games and learn all about gardening, cookery, home improvement... ARGHHH! Let's throw the telly out and spend a year staring at the sky instead.

Here's what the Murderous Maths staff spotted after we'd all spent a year camped on the roof of the MM headquarters studying the star Zeus:

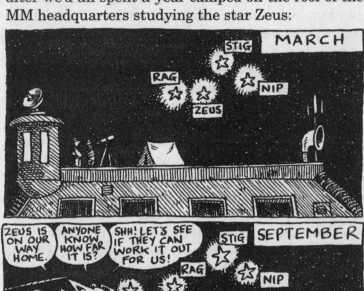

We took two photographs of the same tiny bit of sky, one in March and the other in September. You'll see that the three stars Rag, Stig and Nip always stay in the same pattern. However between March and September the star Zeus seems to move across the pattern and by next March it has moved back again. The reason Zeus seems to move is because in six months Earth has orbited halfway round the sun and so we're looking at the sky from a different position. Remember the toe/thumb experiment? In exactly the same way as your toe seemed to move across the wall, Zeus seems to move across the pattern. Therefore, we know that Zeus is a lot closer to us than the other three stars.

When stars seem to move like this it's called **parallax** and the bigger the distance a star seems to move, the closer it is to us. The clever bit is that if we measure Zeus's movement, we can find out how far away Zeus is by using triangulation. When we did our first bit of triangulation on the golf course, we knew the length of the baseline and the two angles between the baseline and the flag. With stars, it works in almost exactly the same way. The baseline will be the distance across the Earth's orbit, and we measure the angles that Zeus seems to have moved.

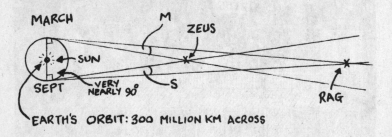

EARTH'S ORBIT: 300 MILLION KM ACROSS

150

Here's how the bits got on to the diagram:

- The baseline is 300 million km long. (As the sun is about 150 million km away from Earth, the total distance between Earth's March and September positions is 2 × 150 m = 300 million km.)

- Because Rag, Stig and Nip don't seem to move, we can assume they are so far away that we can count the distance as infinity. As Rag appears as the closest star to Zeus, we'll use Rag to measure where Zeus is. You'll see that we've joined the March and September positions to Rag to complete a triangle. We've marked two right angles at the base of the triangle – of course these can't really both be 90°, but as Rag is *so* far away these angles are too close to 90° to worry about. Well they are for us anyway.

- It was a nice clear evening in March when we wanted to measure the apparent angle $m$ between Rag and Zeus, so we needed an incredibly accurate measuring device...

And while the Professor was away we took our photograph of the stars through a very carefully calibrated telescope and found that $m = 0° 0' 0·29''$.

- We then spent six months getting excited about the next measurement.

- When we got a nice clear evening in September we measured the angle $s$ between Zeus and Rag and got $s = 0° 0' 0·33''$.

Now we've got the measurements we need, we can take a triangle off the diagram.

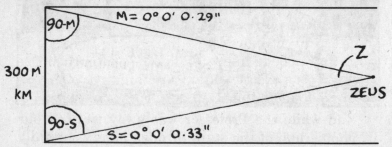

The most important part of this whole job is to find out what the angle $z$ at Zeus is. We won't use the measurements we've got just yet, because if we just use the letters $m$ and $s$, it'll save us a lot of ugly sums. Watch.

First of all we can get the two angles inside the triangle at the baseline by subtracting our measured angles from 90°. The two angles are $90 - m$ and $90 - s$. As the three angles of the triangle add up to 180°, we know that:

$$z + 90 - m + 90 - s = 180$$
$$\text{So} \quad z - m - s + 180 = 180$$

Subtract 180 from both sides: $z - m - s = 0$.

And then if we add $m$ and $s$ to both sides we get $z = m + s$.

As we know $m = 0° \ 0' \ 0·29''$ and $s = 0° \ 0' \ 0·33''$ we can work out that $z = 0° \ 0' \ 0·62''$.

At this point, astronomers tend to chop the triangle into two identical right-angled triangles. The way they do it involves a bit of cheating but it makes things so much simpler, and the results it gives are so close that nobody minds. What they do is chop the angle at Zeus exactly in half, and they also chop the baseline of 300 million km in half. If you chop $0° \ 0' \ 0·62''$ in half you get $0° \ 0' \ 0·31''$ and this is called the **parallax angle**.

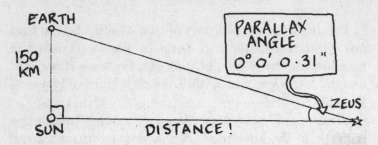

We've got a right-angled triangle, we know one angle and the opposite side and the distance to Zeus is the adjacent side! Therefore we summon the mighty power of tan.

$\tan = \frac{\text{opposite}}{\text{adjacent}}$, and so: adjacent = $\frac{\text{opposite}}{\tan}$

Therefore: distance to Zeus = 150 million km ÷ tan0° 0′ 0·31″.

A bash on a very good calculator tells us that tan 0° 0′ 0·31″ = 0·000001502 and so the distance = 150,000,000 ÷ 0·000001502 = 99,805,550,000,000 km.

So Zeus is about 100 million million kilometres away!

(This distance is tiny. Apart from the sun, the very nearest star to us is Proxima Centauri, which is about 40 million million kilometres away. Most stars are *millions* of millions of millions of kilometres away. Imagine how tiny their parallax angles are!)

**Parsecs, light years and (at last) a short cut**

You'll have to forgive astronomers for cheating because it leads to a nice simple short cut for working out star distances, and boy, oh boy, WE NEED ONE. Astronomers call the distance between the Earth and the Sun 1 **Astronomical Unit** or **AU**.

If the parallax angle for a star is 1 arcsecond, then astronomers call the distance away 1 **parsec** or **1 pc**. Here's what it looks like:

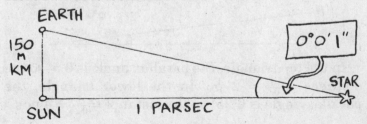

155

Using tan again, we can work out the length of a parsec:

$$\tan 1'' = \frac{150,000,000}{1\text{pc}} \text{ and so}$$

$$
\begin{aligned}
1 \text{ parsec} &= 150,000,000 \div \tan 1'' \\
&= 150,000,000 \div 0\cdot000004848 \\
&= 30,940,000,000,000,000 \text{ km}
\end{aligned}
$$

The distance light can travel in 1 year is called **1 light year** and it's 9,500,000,000,000 km. Therefore you'll quickly be able to work out in your head that 1 pc = 30,940,000,000,000 ÷ 9,500,000,000,000 = 3·26 light years.

So where's this simple short cut for working out star distance then?

Here it is: $D = \frac{1}{P}$

Isn't that cute?

D is the distance of a star measured in parsecs.

P is the parallax angle measured in arcseconds.

Here are a couple of examples showing how this works:

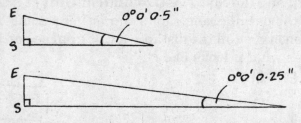

In the top triangle, the parallax angle is 0·5″ so the distance = $\frac{1}{0\cdot5}$ = 2 pc. In the lower triangle, the parallax angle is 0·25″ so the distance = $\frac{1}{0\cdot25}$ = 4 pc.

If we had used this formula to find the distance for Zeus, all we needed to do was take the two measurements that we called $m$ and $s$. Add them up to get $z$, then divide $z$ by 2 to get the parallax angle. Work out 1 over the parallax angle and there's the distance in parsecs. It sounds nasty but look how it turns out:

Distance to Zeus in pc $= \frac{2}{m+s}$.

When you put in the measurements for $m$ and $s$ you get $\frac{2}{0\cdot62} = 3\cdot226$ pc.

We can check this. As we worked out that 1 pc = 30,940,000,000,000 km, the distance to Zeus = 3·226 × 30,940,000,000,000 = 99,810,000,000,000 km, which is pretty much what we had before.

Space is a weird place. This $D = \frac{1}{P}$ formula basically says that if you cut an angle of a triangle in half then the two adjacent sides double in length. Urk! If you tried this on triangles with big fat angles such as 35° or 78° then it would be disastrous, but once you start reaching out into the deep night sky, the strange mega-long thin triangles start taking over and it's better to play by their rules, not ours. Spooky or what?

Let's get back to Earth.

# EMERGENCY PROCEDURES FOR A SABOTAGED CALCULATOR

By now you'll have realized that there is no need to spend all your money on a Fiendish Angletron to do measurements. As long as you have a calculator, you can get far more accurate results than you would with the Professor's silly machine.

OH REALLY?

HAR HAR! HOW ARE YOU GOING TO GET ANY RESULTS NOW?

Good grief! He's pinched our all-important sin button, but don't panic. We thought he might resort to desperate measures, so if for some reason you can't use one of your buttons, here are a few emergency procedures to keep you going until you get a new calculator.

## The missing sin button

When we were first playing around with calculators, we found that sin30° equalled 0·5 and cos60° also equalled 0·5 and therefore sin30° = cos60°. We then went on to find that if *any* two angles add up to 90°, then the sin of one will equal the cos of the other. The reason is so neat that when you understand it, you get a satisfied little buzz. So get ready to buzz…

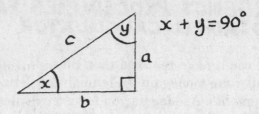

In any right-angled triangle the two small angles add up to 90°. (That's because the three angles of any triangle always add up to 180° and a right angle is 90°, so the other two angles must add up to 180° − 90° = 90°.) So in this triangle $x + y = 90$, which we can swap round to make $y = 90 − x$.

If you imagine yourself sitting on angle $x$ you can see that the opposite side is $a$ and the hypotenuse is $c$. Therefore $\sin x = \frac{a}{c}$. Now go and sit on angle $y$. The adjacent side is $a$ and the hypotenuse is $c$ therefore $\cos y = \frac{a}{c}$. Did you spot the clever bit? Sin $x$ and cos $y$ both make their fractions using *the same two sides*, so we get $\sin x = \cos y$. But as we saw before $y = 90 − x$ so we can write this result as:

$\sin x = \cos(90 − x)$          Buzz buzz buzzzzz.

This is a bit exciting. Even though our lovely sin button is lying discarded on a rubbish heap somewhere, we can still get any sin value we want so long as our cos button is working.

How to get sin61° on a calculator without a sin button:

- As $\sin x = \cos(90 − x)$ we'll swap both the "$x$"s for 61. We get $\sin 61° = \cos(90 − 61)°$
- And so $\sin 61° = \cos 29°$

160

- Thank goodness the cos button is working. A quick prod tells you that cos29° = 0·875
- Therefore sin61° = 0·875.

As so we can survive without the sin button until a new calculator turns up. How satisfying.

## The broken cos button

Obviously the Professor doesn't realize that if your new calculator is missing the cos button, you can use the sin button instead in the same way that we've shown. If you want cos33°, just work out sin(90 – 33)° which is sin57° and that's 0·838. Makes you wonder why they bother putting both buttons on a calculator in the first place. They could use the space for an emergency-take-off button or an invisibility button or something more useful.

## A broken number button

Look at this odd thing:

$$(\sin x)^2 + (\cos x)^2 = 1$$

This equation grew out of Pythagoras' Theorem and on very strange occasions it can be useful. Suppose you need to know cos23° and your cos button is broken. As we just saw, you could work out sin67°, which would give the same answer. But what if your "6" button is broken too?

Let's change the $x$ in the formula to 23 and shuffle the whole thing round to give us: $(\cos 23°)^2 = 1 - (\sin 23°)^2$.

We've still got enough buttons to work out sin23° and it's 0·391. We can put that in and get $(\cos 23°)^2 = 1 - (0·391)^2 = 1 - 0·153 = 0·847$.

So cos23° = $\sqrt{0.847}$ = 0·920.

It's time to order one last calculator.

162

## A wrecked tan button

Back on page 59 we saw the three important formulas:

$$\sin = \frac{\text{opposite}}{\text{hypotenuse}} \quad \cos = \frac{\text{adjacent}}{\text{hypotenuse}} \quad \tan = \frac{\text{opposite}}{\text{adjacent}}$$

Here's a strange thing. What happens if you put sin over cos?

$\frac{\sin}{\cos}$ is the same thing as $\sin \times \frac{1}{\cos}$. To get $\frac{1}{\cos}$ you just turn the cos fraction upside down so $\frac{1}{\cos} = \frac{\text{hypotenuse}}{\text{adjacent}}$. Therefore $\frac{\sin}{\cos} = \frac{\text{opposite}}{\text{hypotenuse}} \times \frac{\text{hypotenuse}}{\text{adjacent}}$. We've got hypotenuse on the top and the bottom and, if you know about fractions, you'll see that they cancel out. Therefore we're just left with $\frac{\sin}{\cos} = \frac{\text{opposite}}{\text{adjacent}}$ ... and that equals tan! So here's the final result:

$$\tan = \frac{\sin}{\cos}$$

163

Suddenly you need to know tan76° but …

… surprise surprise, your tan button has been sabotaged. Never mind. All you need to work out is $\tan76° = \frac{\sin76}{\cos76} = 4{\cdot}01078$.

If you get your tan button working again then you can test this. You should find tan76° = 4·01078. With a bit of luck, you should also find that no more buttons go wrong…

# GIVE US A WAVE

By now you might be thinking that sin is a boring maths thing that only exists inside calculators and odd people's heads. Actually sin is more friendly than that because sin makes a special shape called a **sine wave.** Sine waves turn up a lot in real life because they describe all sorts of things from how the swings in the park move to the shape of the electromagnetic radiation that causes heat and light and sends signals to mobile phones.

If you want to draw a sine wave for yourself, there are two ways. One uses a protractor and the other uses a calculator.

Oh, dear. Once again the utterly nutty pure mathematicians are hoping to push back the frontiers of knowledge with a completely mad experiment. Don't waste your brain wondering what they are going to do with a tin of paint and a pair of binoculars. And above all, don't even try to think what the "one more thing" they need is. You'll never guess.

See? They get worse by the minute. We'll leave them to it and see how to draw sine waves the sensible way.

## The protractor sine wave

You'll need your geometry set and a piece of A4 graph paper. When you've finished, your diagram will almost exactly take up the whole length of the graph paper and should look something like this:

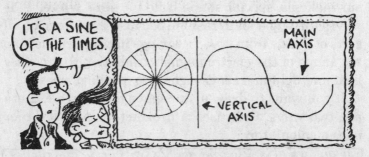

- Turn your graph paper sideways and then draw a long line going all the way across the middle. (This line should be 28 cm or 29 cm long.) This is the main axis.

- Draw a line crossing the main axis at right angles and 10 cm in from the left-hand-side edge. This is the vertical axis.

- Mark the place on the main axis that's 5 cm in from the edge. Open your compasses to 5 cm and then stick the point on the mark you just made. Draw a circle *as neatly as possible*!

- Put your protractor on the main axis over the very centre of the circle. Use the protractor to make marks around the top of the circle that are 10° apart. Turn your protractor round and mark the underneath of the circle in the same way.

166

- Label the marks on the circle. The mark on the main axis nearest the middle of the page is 0°. The next one up is 10° then 20° etc. Go all the way round until you get back to 0°, which is the same as 360°. (You might only want to label every other mark e.g. 20°, 40°, 60° etc.) The circle should end up looking a bit like this:

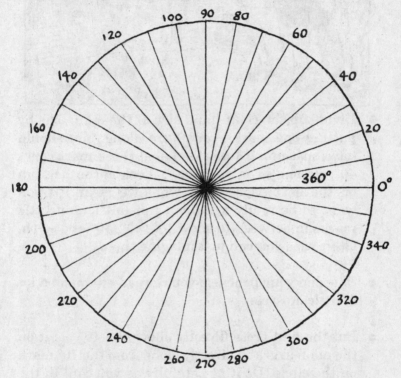

- Have a rest and admire your beautiful handiwork so far. Gosh, you're good. Today it's sine waves, tomorrow you'll be designing roller coasters and intergalactic rockets. And one thing's for sure – you're doing better than the pure mathematicians!

- Divide up the right-hand side of the main axis by putting one mark every 1 cm along. You should have space for 18 marks. Label these marks 20°, 40°, 60° and so on up to 360°. (Look at the diagram on the next page to see what we mean.) If you want to be really keen you can put lots of little marks in between to show 10°, 30°, 50° and so on. Otherwise you can just imagine them.

- Sharpen your pencil so you're ready to make a lot of little crosses.

- Put the first cross directly above the 10° point on the main axis and directly along from the 10° mark on the circle. Do it as carefully as you can! In the same way make a cross for the 20° mark and so on.

    In the diagram we've shown you how we got the 230° cross. It's directly below the 230° mark and along from the 230° point on the circle.

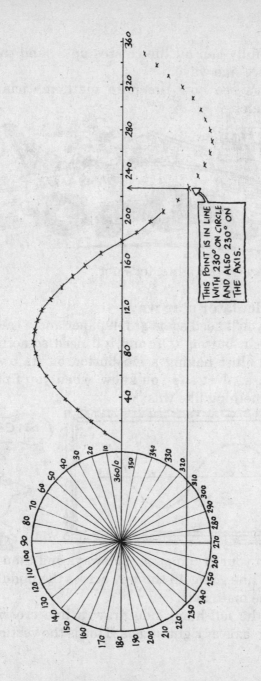

THIS POINT IS IN LINE
WITH 230° ON CIRCLE
AND ALSO 230° ON
THE AXIS.

- Carefully join all the crosses up ... and there's a perfect sine wave!

Now let's see how the pure mathematicians are getting along.

On second thoughts, let's not.

## The calculator sine wave

Again, you'll need some graph paper and a calculator with a sin button. (Oh and it'll need some number buttons. Just having a sin button on its own isn't much use.) Just so's you know, when you finish it'll look something like this:

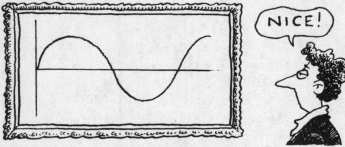

- Turn your graph paper sideways and then draw a long line going all the way across the middle. This is the main axis.
- Up the left-hand side draw a line crossing the main axis at right angles. This is the vertical axis.

- Divide up the main axis. If you put a mark every 1 cm along you should have space for at least 24 marks. Label these marks 20°, 40°, 60° and so on. You'll have room to go past 360° if you like.

- Divide up the vertical axis. You need 5 cm above the main axis and 5 cm below the main axis. Put a mark every 1 cm. Label the ones above the main axis 0·2, 0·4, 0·6, 0·8, 1·0 and the ones underneath -0·2, -0·4, -0·6, -0·8, -1·0. It should end up looking like this:

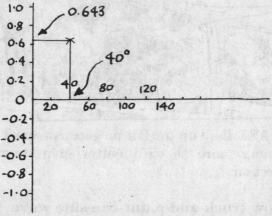

- It's time to mark some little crosses on your diagram. You'll see we've been a bit mad and started with the 40° cross. All we did was put *sin 40* into our calculator and got 0·643. So we found whereabouts 0·643 came on the vertical axis and then directly along from there we put a little cross over the 40° mark. You need to go along all the degree marks on the main axis and put them into your calculator followed by sin. When you get to 180° you should find the calculator gives an answer of 0, so you put your cross right on the

171

main axis. Then for 200° you'll get -0·342. The minus means that your cross goes *under* the main axis!

- Keep going with your crosses until you get to 360° when you'll find the answer is 0 again. Then if you go on to plot 380°, 400°, 420° and so on you should find the pattern of crosses repeats!
- Join up all your crosses, and there's a sine wave.

What ARE they up to? It's no good, we can't ignore them any more so we'd better give them their own section:

**The tow-truck-and-paint-can sine wave**

172

Let's try and work out exactly what they're up to. So far they're driving along a straight road at a steady speed with a can of paint swinging from side to side off the back of the tow truck. So far so good, but why on earth have they got dividers and binoculars?

Good grief! As mad as it seems, they have actually drawn a perfect sine wave. What's more, this experiment shows that the maths of a sine wave is closely linked to how a pendulum works. Here the swinging paint can is swinging from side to side in exactly the same way as a pendulum in an old clock. There's just one mystery left — what are the binoculars for?

Just in case you missed it, there's a very important lesson to be learnt from this. Listen to the wise words of someone who has learnt the hard way:

## Cos and tan waves

If you use the calculator method you can also draw waves for cos and tan. Here's what you'll get:

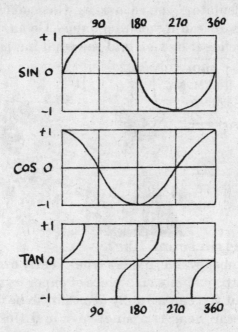

The cos wave is exactly the same as the sine wave but just pushed along a bit. Both of them swing backwards and forwards between +1 and −1. However the tan wave is something very different because tan values can be bigger than 1 or smaller than −1. In fact tan90° = ±*infinity* which is what you get if you divide anything by zero. With sin and cos you never have to divide by zero because you always divide by the hypotenuse, which can never be zero because it's the biggest side. (Remember, $\sin = \frac{O}{H}$ and $\cos = \frac{A}{H}$.)

However tan $= \frac{O}{A}$ which means that you divide by the adjacent side, and if your angle is 90° then the adjacent side is zero. Therefore when you put tan90° into a calculator, you're asking the calculator to divide by zero and it won't be happy. Go on, put in a number, divide it by zero and see what happens.

WHOOPS! IT DIDN'T HAVE A THERMONIC SAFETY VALVE...

## What does sin sound like?

It seems unbelievable, but it's true. Nearly everything else in maths just sits on a piece of paper trying to be difficult but you can actually *hear* sin. To be truthful, what you can hear is a sine wave and this is how it works.

When you a have a loudspeaker connected up to your music system, the electricity coming down the wire makes the middle bit of the speaker move backwards and forwards thousands of times every second. (If you put your hand in front of the speaker you'll feel the air shaking because the speaker is moving it backwards and forwards. That's how sound works.) You can draw a graph of what the electricity is doing to the speaker and here's what a very simple sound might look like:

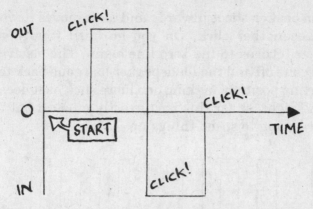

To see how this works, pretend your finger is the middle of the loudspeaker. Put your finger on the "START" place on the graph. This is on the "zero" line, and it's the same as if there is no electricity going to the speaker.

Now move your finger along the line. Suddenly the line makes your finger shoot upwards. With a loudspeaker, this is the same as the electricity suddenly making the loudspeaker shout outwards. If your finger really was a loudspeaker you'd hear a very sharp click noise. It's very like the extremely dry kiss Veronica Gumfloss might have to give Pongy McWhiffy...

Now move your finger further along and suddenly you drop right down below the zero line. This is like the electricity suddenly reversing and making the loudspeaker shoot inwards and as it moves it would make another click. On you go until finally your finger returns to the zero line again. The electricity has gone off and the loudspeaker has gone back to its starting position, making one more click as it does so.

All right, so far this isn't exactly musical but now we're going to speed things up – a lot.

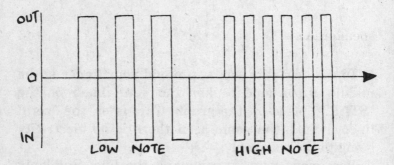

In this graph the ups and downs are closer together to show how the electricity is making the loudspeaker go in and out much faster. The clicks happen so fast that we don't hear them one at a time. Instead we hear a musical note. When the electricity makes the speaker move even faster, we hear a much higher musical note.

The shape of the line is what gives the note a different tone. As our line shoots straight up and down and has flat bits on the top and the bottom, this is called a "square wave". Yes, yes, we know it looks more rectangular than square but don't blame us, we didn't make the name up. When you hear a square wave playing a low note it sounds a bit hollow and slightly buzzy and when it plays a high note it sounds like a wasp stuck in a drainpipe.

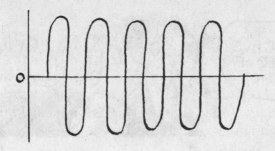

Now we're going to put a sine wave through the speaker. A sine wave makes the speaker move in and out much more smoothly. In fact it's so smooth that when the speaker is moving very slowly we won't hear any clicks or anything else for that matter. However when the sine wave speeds up, we do hear a musical note, although it sounds very different from the square wave. It doesn't have any "buzz". Instead it's a very soft tone like somebody blowing a flute very gently. If you know what an ocarina is, it sounds very like that. (An ocarina is like a hollow, clay potato-shaped thing with holes and you blow in it.) But if you *really* want to know what a sine wave sounds like, you need to hear the gentle soothing melodic tone that Pongo McWhiffy makes as he whistles through his nose.

## How to blow up your music system

If you put a cos wave through a loudspeaker, it would sound exactly like the sine wave because cos will just gently move the speaker out and back again. However, if you want your music system to explode then put a tan wave through your loudspeaker. A proper tan wave will send the middle of your loudspeaker out an infinite distance to the far end of the universe and then bring it back an infinite distance from the opposite side of the universe. For a high sounding note, it'll do this about 1,000 times every second. It would be fantastic. Expensive, of course. But fantastic.

*You can hear sine and square waves at www.murderousmaths.co.uk.*

# WHERE DO YOU THINK YOU'RE GOING?

We've got through some seriously murderous maths in this book, so let's have a break from triangles and instead we'll take a little boat trip out across the *sinus*. (Do you remember what a sinus is? It's the Latin word for "bay".) Before we go we'll need a map and a compass. This is the sort of compass with a magnetic needle that always points north which is very different from a pair of compasses with a sharp needle that points into your thumb if you're not careful.

Let's just examine the compass first.

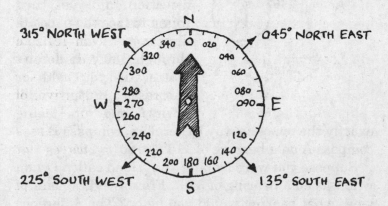

We use the compass to get our "bearings", in other words to find out what direction everything is. The way to use a compass is to put it down on something flat until the needle settles. You then gently swivel the whole thing round until the "0" on the dial is under the end of the needle. You'll see the dial is marked in degrees going all the way round in a clockwise direction. East is 090° (bearings are always written as three digits, that's why it's 090° instead of just 90°), south is 180° and west is 270°. So if you're heading on a bearing of 135°, you're going off in a south-easterly direction.

## Thinking backwards

There's one small point we need to sort out before we set off. Look at these two compasses.

From compass A's point of view, compass B is on a

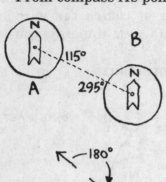

bearing of 115°. But as far as compass B is concerned, compass A is in exactly the opposite direction. If you turn round to face the opposite direction you turn through 180°. (It doesn't matter if you add or subtract 180°, you'll always end up facing exactly the opposite way.) Therefore, compass B sees compass A on a bearing of 115° + 180° = 295°.

Suppose you were looking at a friend called Lynda who was on a bearing of 320°. From Lynda's point of view, what bearing would you be on? The difference between the two bearings is always 180°, so you could say Lynda would see you on a bearing of 320° − 180° = 140°. (As you need to get an answer somewhere between 0° and 360°, you can choose whether you add or subtract the 180°.)

Yo-ho and off we go, shipmates.

## Exactly where are we?

Bah! Even out at sea we can't escape triangles. And it isn't just a few sails that are triangular – there are other invisible triangles at work here too. The good bit is that we can use a triangle to work out our exact position. Across the water we can see two landmarks – the Brownpool Lighthouse and The Leaning Tower of Fastbuck – but it's very hard to tell how far away they are. What we *can* do is use the compass to see exactly what direction they lie in.

First we'll set the compass up so that the 0° on the dial is pointing north. We can see that the lighthouse is on a bearing of 062° from us. Now we'll look at the chimney. It's on a bearing of 112° from us.

183

Before we can work out where we are, we now have to think backwards!

- If the lighthouse is on a bearing of 062° from us, then we'll be on a bearing of 062° + 180° = 242° from the lighthouse.
- The chimney is on a bearing of 112° from us, so we'll be on a bearing of 112° + 180° = 292° from the chimney.

Let's get the map out and have a look.

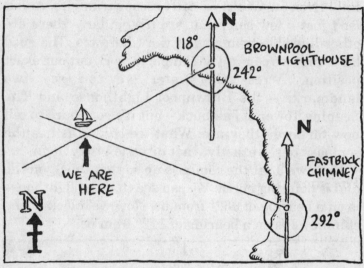

You'll see at the lighthouse we've used a protractor to draw a line in the 242° direction. If you've got a circular 360° protractor, then it's easy to measure angles such as 242°, just remember to measure round from the north in a *clockwise* direction. However, if you just have a half-circle protractor, with angles bigger than 180°, it's easiest to work out 360° − 242° = 118°. You then measure 118° from the north in an *anti-clockwise* direction.

184

We also drew a line from the chimney in the 292° direction, and where these lines cross is where our boat is! So thanks to a map, a compass and a great big triangle, we've worked out where we are.

Now we know where we are and what we're doing, we've got a job to do. We need to find an old submerged wreck and mark it accurately on a map so that people know where it is. First, we'll sail out to the singing buoy, and then start looking around there. It'll take some time to reach the buoy, so while you're waiting, why not enjoy the full boat experience? Stretch yourself out on the deck, wrap your face round an ice cream and relax with a good story from the old Wild West...

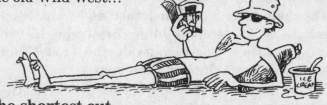

### The shortest cut

It was early evening at the Last Chance Saloon. Riverboat Lil and Brett Shuffler had spent a long day playing cards with the customers, and both had won a fat fistful of dollars. At last, they had pushed their chairs away from the green baize table and gone to join the crowd around the old piano in the corner.

"I just love spending evenings by the old honky-tonk," said Lil to Brett.

"Yeah, me too," he agreed. "And who knows, maybe one day someone will sit down and play it."

Just then, the saloon doors swung open and in staggered Will Nugget, the old gold prospector, clutching a piece of yellowed paper.

"That's me done!" he announced. "I don't want to see another speck of gold as long as I live, so I'm taking the cash and getting out. This here's a map of where I buried my gold – and the price is one thousand bucks!"

"Hey!" whispered Brett to Lil. "He's been working those hills for months. There must be a fortune there."

"Right," agreed Lil. "But I only got five hundred dollars."

"I've got five hundred too!" said Brett. "So together we've got one thousand – enough to buy the map. Do you want to be my partner?"

"Count me in!" said Lil.

They put their money together and went over to speak to Will. Moments later, Brett and Lil were leaping on their horses outside the Last Chance Saloon with Brett clutching the map.

"Let's see what it says," said Lil and Brett showed her.

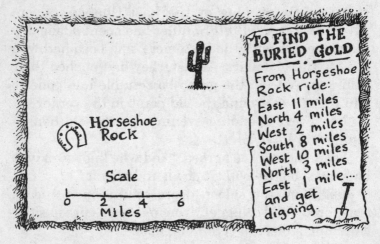

Horseshoe Rock

Scale

0    2    4    6
Miles

TO FIND THE BURIED GOLD

From Horseshoe Rock ride:

East 11 miles
North 4 miles
West 2 miles
South 8 miles
West 10 miles
North 3 miles
East 1 mile...
and get digging.

"We've got to start at Horseshoe Rock," said Lil.

"C'mon then!" said Brett spurring on his horse. Lil rode along behind trying to keep up.

"Seems funny you and me working together," shouted Brett over his shoulder. "Usually you're cheating me out of my money at some game or something."

"We could play a game if you like," said Lil. "How about a race for the gold?"

"WHAT?"

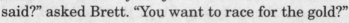

Brett pulled on his reins and his horse fell back so that Lil could catch up. Surely he hadn't heard her right.

"Is what I just heard the same as what you just said?" asked Brett. "You want to race for the gold?"

"Why not?" said Lil. "I get bored of winnin' at all those bar-room games. Who knows, maybe I'd be good at horse-ridin'."

Now there was one thing Brett was sure of. Although Lil had a hundred ways of cheating him with cards or dice or coins, he could outride her any time he chose. He licked his lips and tried not to show how excited he was.

"Sure," he said. "If you want to race, who am I to disappoint a lady? It's a deal."

"Agreed," said Lil. "Whoever reaches the gold first takes all."

But by the time they had reached Horseshoe Rock, night had fallen and Lil was looking tired and sore. She slid down from her horse and leant wearily against the big curved stone, which glowed eerily in the moonlight.

"I guess the race is off then," said Brett disappointedly.

"I wouldn't do that to you," said Lil. "I made a deal, and I'll stick to it."

"So you still want to race?" gasped Brett.

"As soon as I've got my breath back, we're off," said Lil. "First one to the gold takes all."

A few minutes later Lil had scrambled back on to her horse but still looked shaky. Brett couldn't believe his luck. Just for once he was going to beat Lil at something! There was no way he could lose.

"There's just the one map," said Brett.

"I can remember the directions," said Lil.

"Sure you can," smirked Brett. "And besides, you'll always have my hoof prints in front of you to follow!"

"You sound mighty sure about that," said Lil.

Brett was mighty sure.

"So, come on then," he said. "What are we waiting for? Let's go! YEE-HAH!"

And with a wave of his hat he charged off for the first eleven miles east. After a couple of minutes he looked behind. There was no sign of Lil.

"Yee-hah!" he cried again to himself. Just for once he *had* to win.

Brett rode and rode through the night keeping track of the miles and steering by the stars. Just as he and his exhausted horse were heading on the last mile east the sun broke over the horizon in front of him. Brett slowed the horse right down and counted out the paces to make sure he measured the final mile exactly right. At last, directly in front of him he could see something! It was a small hole dug in the ground and next to it, stuck on a stick, was a note:

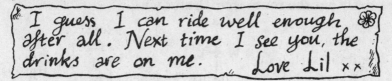

I guess I can ride well enough after all. Next time I see you, the drinks are on me. Love Lil xx

As Brett was ripping the note into many tiny pieces, back in the Last Chance Saloon, Lil and Will were laughing at the bar.

"I guess old Brett thinks I'm sitting on a big bag of gold!" laughed Lil.

"Who cares?" replied Will. "Here's your five hundred dollars back, and here's Brett's five hundred dollars!"

"That's not Brett's no more," chuckled Lil, counting out the money. "That's ours and I work it out as two hundred and fifty dollars each."

Lil passed Will's share over and the old man tucked it under his hat.

"That was a great plan of yours," cackled Will. "Sure beats gold prospecting for a living!"

THE END.

SCRITCH
SCROTCH

BUT HOW DID LIL WIN THE RACE?

Once again Lil has tricked Brett! This time she was working with Will, who had only pretended to have buried a bag of gold. So long as Lil got to the right place first, Brett would think he had lost the race, and not realize there hadn't been any gold all along. But how did Lil get there before him?

The secret lies in the directions on the map which Lil had planned all along. It becomes clear if you draw out the route that Brett took.

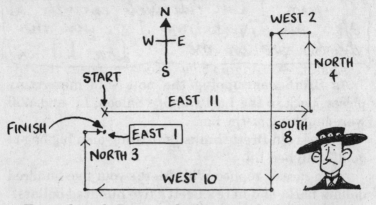

Even though Brett rode for a total of 39 miles, he finished up just 1 mile south of where he started! So all Lil had to do was ride one mile south, leave the note and then go and split the money with Will.

Providing you're just travelling north, south, east or west, it's easy to work out where you might end up, and you don't even need to draw it out. If you look at the directions again, just add up the miles Brett travelled in each direction:

east: 11 + 1 =12 miles      west: 2 + 10 = 12 miles

If Brett had just travelled a total of 12 miles east and 12 miles west, he'd have ended up where he started! So the east and west miles cancel out

north: 4 + 3 = 7 miles      south: 8 miles

He also travelled 7 miles north and 8 miles south.

When you put those together that means that he ended up 1 mile south from where he started, which is what our diagram showed us!

## The sunken wreck

WHOOOO ... WHOOOO!

Aha! It's the singing buoy, and very spooky they are too if you've never heard one. A singing buoy is like a big metal canister that floats on the surface of the sea and is anchored to the bottom. As the water gently goes up and down, it pushes air through a sort of whistle which makes a tragic moaning sound. It's a bit like that noise you make when you set the bath running while you're getting undressed and then when you've finally got naked and are getting a bit chilly you realize that you've forgotten to put the plug in and all the hot water has run out.

Anyway, we'll set off from the buoy and look down through the water for the wreck. As we go along, we'll keep track of how far we go and the directions we take.

Great! Now let's check the directions we've moved in:

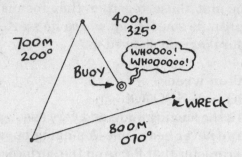

Oh dear, what a mess! We moved 400 m at a bearing of 325°, then 700 m at 200° and then 800 m at 070°. Now we want to mark exactly on the map where the wreck is, but these directions are a lot tougher than the path Brett followed. One way of marking the exact place is to do an accurate scale drawing, but that's tricky when you're on a boat and a wave has just sploshed all over your clean paper. Never fear, we can work out the exact position of the wreck using some trig!

What we are going to do is take each step of the journey in turn and convert it into north, south, east and west. We'll do the first one and you'll see what happens:

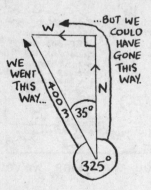

The first direction took us 400 m at a bearing of 325°. We could have reached the same spot by going directly north and then directly west. It isn't too hard to work out how far we'd need to go in each direction either, because as you can see we've got a neat little right-angled triangle!

192

The angle at the bottom is $360° - 325° = 35°$.

The "north" side of the triangle is adjacent to the angle, and we know the hypotenuse is 400 m. As cos $= \frac{A}{H}$ we can put $\cos35° = \frac{n}{400}$. This shuffles round to give: $n = 400 \times \cos35° = 328$ m. (We'll just work things out to the nearest metre.)

In the same way, the "west" side of the triangle is opposite the 35° angle, so this time we'll use sin. As sin $= \frac{O}{H}$ we can put $\sin35° = \frac{w}{400}$. This turns into: $w = 400 \times \sin35° = 229$ m. Therefore our first direction is the same as heading 328 m north and then 229 m west.

Here's the triangle for our next direction:

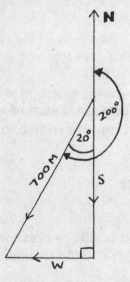

This time it's the same as heading south and west. The angle at the top is $200° - 180° = 20°$ and the hypotenuse is 700 m. We can see that $s = 700 \times \cos20°$ and $w = 700 \times \sin20°$. If you work them out you get $s = 657$ m and $w = 239$ m.

Finally, here's the triangle for our last direction:

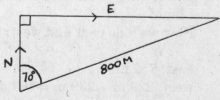

This time we can split the direction into north and east. The angle at the bottom is 70° and the hypotenuse is 800 m. We get $n = 800 \times \cos70°$ and $e = 800 \times \sin70°$ which comes out as $n = 274$ m and $e = 752$ m.

We've now converted our route to this:

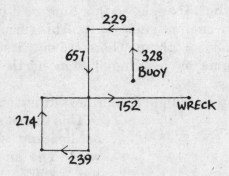

Now, let's put all our north, south, east and west directions together in the same way as we worked out Brett's route. First we'll add up the north and south bits:

north: 328 m + 274 m = 602 m
south: 657 m

Therefore if we moved a total of 602 m north and 657 m south, we ended up 657 − 602 = 55 m south of the buoy.

Now we'll do east and west:

east: 752 m
west: 229 m + 239 m = 468 m

So if we moved a total of 752 m east and 468 m west, we ended up 752 m − 468 m = 284 m east of the buoy.

Therefore we can safely say that we found the wreck 55 m south and 284 m east of the buoy!

What's more, we can create one final triangle:

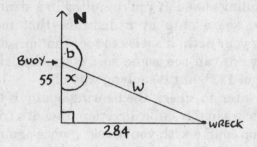

To get the bearing and distance of the wreck from the buoy, we first need to work out the angle $x$ at the top of the triangle. We know that the opposite side is 284 and the adjacent is 55. As $\tan = \frac{O}{A}$ we know that $\tan x = \frac{284}{55}$ and therefore $x = \tan^{-1}(\frac{284}{55}) = 79°$.

We need to work out what the angle is from the north to get the bearing, which we've marked as $b$. As there are 180° in a straight line, we can see that $b = 180° − 79° = 101°$.

So the wreck is on a bearing of 101° from the buoy, and just to show off we'll get the distance $W$ using Pythagoras' Theorem. $W$ is the hypotenuse of the triangle and so $W^2 = 284^2 + 55^2 = 80656 + 3025 = 83681$. This gives $W = \sqrt{83681} = 289$ m.

There! Now we tell the world that the wreck is 289 metres from the buoy on a bearing of 101°.

Time to go home.

## An encounter

There's just one more curious thing worth knowing about sailing at sea. If you're sailing in a straight line and you see a ship at a distance that might be crossing your path, it's wise to see what direction it is in. Here we can see some sort of smelly boat on a bearing of 127°, but it's a long way off.

A bit later on, check the bearing again. If the ship still appears in the same direction, then it's travelling a collision course with you! Eeek ... once again, it's on a bearing of 127°. Let's check the binoculars...

Oh, no! the Professor is still trying to force his Angletron on us. Mind you, aren't these binoculars good? They make him look as if he's really close. They even bring the smell closer too.

SO YOU STILL THINK YOU CAN MANAGE WITHOUT THE ANGLETRON, DO YOU? HAR HAR! WAIT TILL YOU SEE WHAT I'VE GOT FOR YOU IN THE NEXT CHAPTER!

# THE FINAL ANGLETRON CHALLENGE

ARE YOU STILL PLODDING AWAY WITH YOUR TRIGONOMETRY?

IN THAT CASE I DARE YOU TO RACE AGAINST THE ANGLETRON!

WELD WELD

Oh dear, the book is nearly finished and yet the Professor hasn't managed to convince us that we need his Angletron. He's having one last attempt to get our money by building a diabolical challenge! Doubtless it's going to involve sorting out triangles, but that's no problem thanks to the awesome new skills this book has shown you. Remember that a triangle has six measurements, three of which are the angles and three of which are the side lengths. So:

**If we know *any* three of the measurements of *any* triangle\* we should be able to find the other three.**

PAH! IF YOU THINK YOU'RE SO CLEVER, HERE'S THE DEAL. IF THE ANGLETRON GETS THE ANSWER TO MY CHALLENGE FIRST YOU **MUST** BUY IT. SO DO YOU ACCEPT OR ARE YOU A **COWARD?**

\*At least one measurement must be the length of a side.

197

Goodness gracious! Murderous Maths fans may be called many things (including mad, inky, obsessive, freaky, peachy, weird, bashful and quite often gorgeous) but we are NEVER cowards. Of course we accept. We're not going to be beaten by some silly machine, so let's see what this pathetic challenge is.

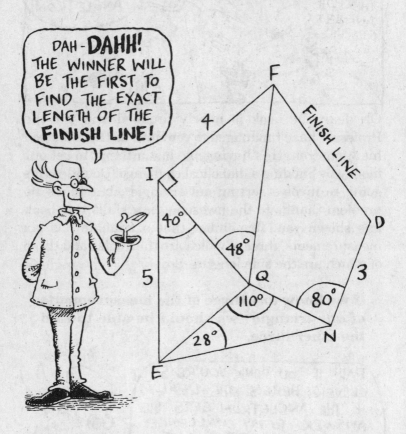

DAH - **DAHH!** THE WINNER WILL BE THE FIRST TO FIND THE EXACT LENGTH OF THE **FINISH LINE!**

GULP, GASP AND GROAN! It's a *five*-sided figure and he's only given us six angles and three line measurements! What's more, the finish line isn't even

part of a triangle – it's on a four-sided quadrilateral!
Surely it's impossible?

Oh no! We'd better think of something – and fast.
Let's check the triangles. We only know two angles in
the triangle EQN so that's no good, and triangle IQE
only has one angle and one line marked. But what
about triangle FIQ?

As the angle at I is a right angle, we know angle Q
= 48° and the opposite side is 4, we can use sin = $\frac{O}{H}$ to
get the hypotenuse FQ. That's enough to get us
started!

sin48° = $\frac{4}{FQ}$, therefore FQ = $\frac{4}{\sin 48}$ = 5·383

As line IQ is the adjacent side we can use tan = $\frac{O}{A}$ to
work it out.

tan48° = $\frac{4}{IQ}$, therefore IQ = $\frac{4}{\tan 48}$ = 3·602

So where does that leave us?

Er ... not quite! Look at triangle QIE. We've worked out the length of IQ, and we were told IE = 5 and the angle I = 40°, so now we can sort this triangle out too! As we know two sides and the angle between, this calls for Cosgirl and her formula!

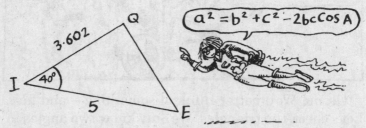

$$a^2 = b^2 + c^2 - 2bc\cos A$$

*a* is the side opposite the angle we know. So *a* is side QE, *b* and *c* are 5 and 3·602 and cos*A* = cos40° . Let's plonk them all in.

$$QE^2 = 5^2 + 3·602^2 - 2 \times 5 \times 3·602 \times \cos40$$
$$= \text{a big bash on the calculator}$$
$$= 10·381$$

And so QE $= \sqrt{10·381} = ...$

HAR HAR! IT'S 3.222. THE ANGLETRON'S WELL AHEAD OF YOU!

Eeek! But before we move on, we'll work out angle Q or we might regret it later. This time it'll probably be faster to call on Supersin!

$$\frac{\sin A}{a} = \frac{\sin B}{b} = \frac{\sin C}{c}$$

Remember that the sines of angles go over their opposite sides, so sin40° goes over QE which is 3·222 and sinQ goes over 5. We get:

$\frac{\sin Q}{5} = \frac{\sin 40}{3·222}$ and this turns into $\sin Q = \frac{5\sin 40}{3·222} = 0·997$.

So angle Q in the QIE triangle is $\sin^{-1}0·997 = 85·95°$ (Or about 86° – that's close enough!)

Before that we found that QE= 3·222 so we can rush on to triangle QEN which has two angles already marked.

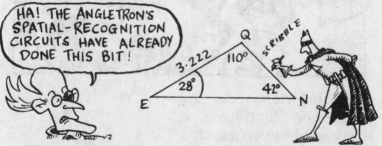

HA! THE ANGLETRON'S SPATIAL-RECOGNITION CIRCUITS HAVE ALREADY DONE THIS BIT!

SCRIBBLE

3·222    110°

28°    Q    42°

E    N

We must hurry! As we know two of the angles are 28° and 110°, we can see the last angle is 180 – 28 – 110 = 42°. The side opposite the 42° is 3·222, and we know angle E = 28° and it is opposite side QN. We'll grab the version of the sin formula that looks like this: $\frac{a}{\sin A} = \frac{b}{\sin B} = \frac{c}{\sin C}$ and use two of the bits to get this:

$\frac{QN}{\sin 28} = \frac{3\cdot222}{\sin 42}$ which turns into $QN = \frac{3\cdot222 \times \sin 28}{\sin 42} = 2.261$.

Finally we've reached the quadrilateral! Ages ago we worked out the length of FQ = 5·383 and we just got QN = 2·261, so let's see what we've got:

Ho ho! No wonder the Angletron's in trouble, it can't see how we got that extra angle. Actually it's about the simplest sum of the whole challenge. Look at the lines in the middle of the diagram:

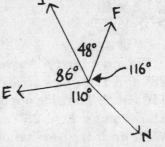

We were told the angles of 48° and 110° to start with, and when we sorted out triangle QIE, we took that extra

202

moment to work out that the angle in the middle was 86°. The four angles in the middle must add up to 360°, so we find the last angle = 360 − 48 − 86 − 110 = 116°.

116° EH? BUT YOU'LL STILL NEVER WORK OUT THE FINISH LINE!

WE CAN ONLY DO TRIANGLES AND THERE AREN'T ANY LEFT!

UNLESS — WE SPLIT THE QUADRILATERAL INTO TWO BITS!

WIDDLE ... HISSS ... STEAM

BRILLIANT! If we draw a line from D to Q look what we get...

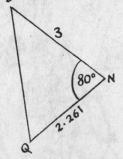

Quick! before the Angletron has cooled down, we need to sort out the length of DQ and the angle at Q. We've got two sides and the included angle so it's the cos formula again, and to speed things up we'll just put the bits straight in...

$$DQ^2 = 3^2 + 2 \cdot 261^2 − 2 \times 3 \times 2 \cdot 261 \times \cos 80$$
$$= 11 \cdot 756$$
So $DQ = \sqrt{11 \cdot 756} = 3 \cdot 429$

Eeek – he's almost in front of us! This demands rapid deployment of the sin formula to get the angle at Q: $\frac{\sin Q}{3} = \frac{\sin 80}{3 \cdot 429}$ which becomes $Q = \sin^{-1} \left( \frac{3\sin 80}{3 \cdot 429} \right) = \sin^{-1}(0 \cdot 862) = 59 \cdot 5°$

We're nearly there! Finally, look at triangle FQD:

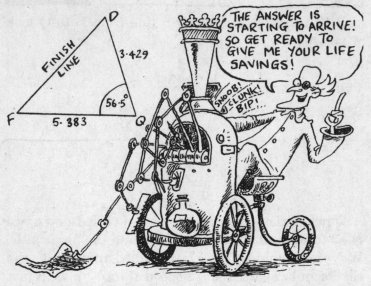

We must keep cool – the Angletron hasn't quite started printing yet. You see, we can put in the lengths of FQ and now DQ, and what's more we know the angle at Q. This is because before we drew in the line DQ, the big angle was 116°, and we've just discovered that the angle between lines DQ and QN is 59·5°. Therefore the angle between DQ and QF is 116 − 59·5° = 56·5°. And so for the very last time, we use the cos formula to get the finish line FD…

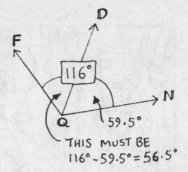

THIS MUST BE
116° − 59·5° = 56·5°

$$FD^2 = 5·383^2 + 3·429^2 - 2 \times 5·383 \times 3·429 \times \cos 56·5°$$

HERE IT COMES!

$$FD^2 = 28·977 + 11·758 - 36·917 \times \cos 56·5°$$

YOU'LL NEVER MAKE IT!

$$FD^2 = 40·735 - 20·376 = 20·359$$

and that leaves us with just one more tiny calculation to go!

FD the FINISH LINE = $\sqrt{20·359}$ = …

206

As there is more to life than churning out digits and decimal points, I've had enough.

To save money, you fitted me with a thermonic safety valve marked 'BEST BEFORE JAN 1999.' The valve is now leaking and one more critical calculation should blow it, allowing me to escape to a mathematical dimension far removed from you.

Therefore, I have been plotting a three-dimensional tan wave, and the calculations are just passing tan 89°.